SECOND CHANCE

Additional copies of this book are available from two locations:
Adventist Book Centers: Call **1-800-765-6955**.
or visit **adventistbookcenter.com**
3ABN: Call **1-800-752-3226** or visit **www.3abn.org**

Review and Herald® titles may be purchased in bulk for educational, business, fund-raising, or sales promotional use. For information, e-mail SpecialMarkets@reviewandherald.com.

From a life of drugs,
crime, and misery...

SECOND CHANCE

...to worldwide ministry

REVIEW AND HERALD® PUBLISHING ASSOCIATION
Since 1861 | www.reviewandherald.com

3ABN BOOKS
Three Angels Broadcasting Network
West Frankfort, Illinois
www.3abn.org

Published by Review and Herald® Publishing Association, Hagerstown, MD 21741-1119

The Review and Herald® Publishing Association publishes biblically based materials for spiritual, physical, and mental growth and Christian discipleship.

3ABN BOOKS is dedicated to bringing you the best in published materials consistent with the mission of Three Angels Broadcasting Network. Our goal is to uplift Jesus through books, audio, and video materials by our family of 3ABN presenters. Our in-depth Bible study guides, devotionals, biographies, and lifestyle materials promote the whole person in health and the mending of broken people. For more information call 616-627-4651 or visit 3ABN's web site: www.3ABN.org

The author assumes full responsibility for the accuracy of all facts and quotations as cited in this book.

This book was
Edited by Penny Estes Wheeler
Copyedited by James Hoffer
Cover designed by Chrystique "CQ" Neibauer/cqgraphicdesign.com
Interior designed by Tina M. Ivany
Cover photos by Jim Ayer and Shutterstock
Typeset: Bembo 10.5/12.5

PRINTED IN U.S.A.
14 13 12 11 10 5 4 3 2 1

Library of Congress Cataloging-in-Publication Data
Ayer, Jim, 1948- .
Second chance : from a life of drugs, crime, and misery. . . to worldwide ministry / Jim Ayer ; with Maylan Schurch.
p. cm.
1. Ayer, Jim, 1948- 2. Seventh-Day Adventists—Biography. I. Schurch, Maylan. II. Title.
BX6193.A94A3 2010
286.7'32092—dc22
[B]

2009037310

ISBN 978-0-8280-2492-1

ACKNOWLEDGEMENTS

As you will soon realize, I am a type AAA personality. My wife, Janene, realized that fact too late. But after she said "I do" many years ago, she has been a wonderfully faithful and tremendous partner, and I couldn't get along without her!

Thank you, honey!

Special love goes to my mom and dad, who had to put up with years of my wanderings. And until they read this book, they didn't realize how many wanderings that was. No one could have better parents.

Some of those affected by my wanderings from the Lord were our children, Dan, Jason, and Meriah. To you I want to say I'm sorry. But praise God through His sacrifice and power He offers us victory! I love you very much and am looking forward to spending eternity with each one of you.

To list and thank everyone who has been a positive influence in my life leading to the writing of this book would be almost impossible but I've got to share some of them with you.

Thank you, Jeannette Johnson and Doug Sayles of the Review and Herald for the encouragement to put my story on paper.

And finally, to Maylan Schurch: Without you there would be no polish or shine within these pages. It's amazing how God used us to touch your heart more than 35 years ago, but we wouldn't have known it if we had not worked on this book together.

CONTENTS

FOREWORD

What an inspirational story you are about to read! From being high on drugs in San Francisco's hippie culture to experiencing God's ultimate high—the satisfaction that can come only by sharing salvation with a lost and dying world. Your heart will be touched as you read this amazing testimony, from the love of Jungle Jim's exotic animals to preaching God's love in exotic places; from being bound by addictions to living a life of total surrender.

I personally connected with this book because Jim and I share similar stories. When we are willing to listen to the Voice—as Jim calls God's calling—and step out of our comfort zone to be used of God, awesome things happen. I went from being a battered wife to being blessed with an incredible worldwide television ministry. Jim went from living a drug-battered life to leading out in an amazing worldwide radio ministry that is winning souls in places only shortwave radio can enter.

I get excited every time I hear the testimony of someone fully surrendered to God for I know by personal experience that nothing in life brings more personal pleasure than stepping out in faith and letting God lead.

Whether your prayer is like mine, "Lord, please use me in a special way," or Jim's, "Lord, let me win the world for You," God has an incredible journey planned for your life. All it takes is your willingness to surrender all and let Him take the driver's seat. When you do, hang on! You'll experience the most thrilling joyride you could ever imagine.

I can promise you one thing as you read how God changed a man, his wife, his friends, and the strangers he touched—you will never again be the same. You will yearn for the same powerful prayer life that broke Satan's hold on Jim's selfish heart, brought him to the foot of the cross, and gave him the abundant life that Jesus promised. And when that happens to you, watch out. God will use you in an incredible way, too.

—Brenda Walsh
Producer/Host
3ABN's "Kids Time"

But as it is written:
"Eye has not seen, nor ear heard,
Nor have entered into the heart of man
The things which God has prepared for those who love Him."

—1 Corinthians 2:9

If you have used a GPS (Global Positioning System) you know that even if you miss the correct turn it automatically recalculates and again points you toward your destination.

I missed dozens of turns, and some even brought me close to death. But God's GPS kept bringing me back on track.

CHAPTER 1:

A SHORT TIME TO DECIDE

You want high, Jim Ayer? God rumbled. *I'll show you high.*

I'm putting words in His mouth, of course. I didn't hear Him say anything—at that point. I didn't even believe in God. But both those sentences ended up being true. I did want to get high, and God showed me a *real* high.

It was 1967, and I was 19 years old. Perched on the edge of my unmade bed in a postage-stamp-size rented room in Mount Shasta, California, I inserted a smoldering marijuana joint between my lips.

I'll show you high.

Three long drags and I was feeling the familiar buzz. After all, I was a hippie's hippie. A commune in San Francisco's Haight-Ashbury was where I'd bought my drugs when I lived in Oakland the year before. I'd been not only a user but also a dealer, and had convinced dozens of other kids to try drugs by telling them about the "higher plane of existence" these drugs would open to them.

I'll show you high, Jim Ayer!

I stared at the floor, and inhaled again. To my surprise, the floor fell away from beneath me and widened into a basketball court far below. The walls and ceiling also expanded, and suddenly I was *really* high—sitting on the top tier in a huge stadium, the bleachers sloping dizzyingly down in front of me.

But though the polished floor far below gleamed in the spotlights, I saw no basketball team. Instead, a small table stood at center court, and in chairs on either side two men sat facing each other. I was too far away to see them clearly, but each looked impressively powerful. And with weird certainty, I knew exactly who they were.

That one is God, I thought. *And the other is the devil.*

I could hear them speaking, their voices echoing in the empty stadium. I don't remember all their words, but I do know whom they were talking about—*me.* My life was on the line. God and Satan were discussing my destiny.

I almost said *arguing* my destiny, but it wasn't really an argument. In tones which made me shudder, the devil would claim me as his servant, but God would calmly respond, and whatever He said made the devil fall silent.

Gathering his thoughts, Satan would lay out more reasons why I should belong to him, using the same lines of reasoning I'd used to talk everyone I came in contact with into doing drugs. I heard phrases like "expanded mind" and "heightened consciousness."

The master deceiver had written my playbook, my whole script, the words I used to bring as many people as possible down to the pit . . . the pit I was in. Could he have used these ideas when talking Eve into taking a bite of the mind-expanding forbidden fruit? *Come on, Eve. Try it. Just once. You will be like God . . .*

But God wasn't buying the devil's line. From His side of the table He said something emphatic and powerful yet calm, and again the devil went silent.

How long I gazed at that awesome spectacle I don't know. But suddenly, in an eyeblink, the floor swooped up, the walls telescoped inward, and I was back on my bed in my postage-stamp room.

But no marijuana-buzz lingered. I'd gone stone-cold sober.

"What's going on?" I muttered. "I've never had that kind of trip before. And who was this God? Who was this devil? And why did I know them?"

"Jim," said a clear, strong voice very close to me.

I glanced around. I was alone.

"Jim!" The voice crackled with authority. *"You have a short time to decide."*

Deciding—wisely—hadn't been one of my strengths to this point. Unlike a lot of less fortunate kids of my generation, I can't blame Mom and Dad for my daily marijuana joint. (I can't even blame the name of the California town I where I was born, "Weed"!)

For one thing, my dad had set me a totally different example. Not only was he a hard-working timber-faller, braving daily danger to put food on the table. He'd also been a World War II soldier attached to the 101st Airborne Division. And three years before I was born, something happened to him that could have made things a lot different for me if they'd gone wrong.

In December 1944 Dad and his company found themselves in the little Belgian town of Bastogne surrounded by Hitler's troops. The German army wanted that town—a key transportation artery—and their forces relentlessly pounded the 101st in what would become known as the Battle of the Bulge.

While it was daylight, American aircraft beat back the enemy. But when the American planes left, the Germans would get revenge by sending in the Luftwaffe, bombing and strafing all night long. Dad and his company needed a safe place to get some sleep, and they thought they'd finally found it in the basement of an old church where they bedded down to get what rest they could.

Suddenly, above them, they heard a horrific smashing of stone and snapping of timbers.

"Bomb!" someone screamed.

Everybody grabbed their flashlights and scrambled upward through the rubble.

"It hasn't gone off yet!" someone else shouted. "Run!"

The only way out was past the massive 500-pound explosive. *It's gotta be on a fuse,* Dad thought, *or a timer. Or is it a dud?* He was about to take to his heels when he noticed a crack in the bomb's casing, and what looked like powder was pouring out onto the floor. Dad reached down, grabbed a fistful, and dashed out to take cover with his buddies. Palms over their ears, they waited.

"It's a dud," someone said a minute or two later.

"Look at this," Dad said, opening his fist and showing his buddies the grainy substance in his hand. "Give me a cigarette lighter and let's see what happens." Carefully he tried to light a few grains, but nothing happened.

"It looks like sand," someone said.

"It *is* sand!" Dad said.

"But who would put sand in a bomb?" a young recruit asked, bewildered.

"A saboteur," an older soldier replied promptly. "Once in a while the Germans use prisoners of war in their bomb-making factories. Maybe a Yank or a Brit or a Pole got the job of filling this bomb, and shoveled in sand instead. Just doing his bit for the war effort."

It still amazes me to think that the reason I was even born and able to write this is that a prisoner of war, forced to work in a German factory long ago and far away, cared so much for people he would never meet that he risked his life to disable a German bomb.

Just fate?

I don't think so.

Dad made it home in once piece and started his family. I was born on a cold January day into a happy home. Like most kids, my earliest memories are dramatic ones, such as the time I saw a cat walking past a window and threw a pair of pliers at it. I missed the cat, but scored a direct hit on the window.

Or the time my parents discovered me enveloped me in a brilliant flame of light, caused when my 5-year-old hand gripped a screwdriver and thrust it into a 220-volt kitchen stove socket. I was also 5 when, using a paint roller and a can of fire engine red, I helpfully painted the beautiful wooden walls of our guest cabin as high as I could reach.

"Go to your room!" Mom hissed. "Right now!"

Later she told me why she chose that punishment. "I was so mad," she confessed, "that I was afraid I'd do something to you I'd be sorry for later."

And I can't say I began using drugs because I was a spoiled kid. Mom and Dad barely had enough money to survive, let alone spoil me. When popular singer Tennessee Ernie Ford sang—the song that contained the line "I owe my soul to the company store!"—he was singing about the life and times of my mom and dad's post-Depression era. My mom started working for the company store shortly after she was married at age 16. I was born much later, but the company store was still the place to go in town. I loved going to it. It was Walmart on a smaller scale, especially to the excited eyes of a 7-year-old.

Our home had no real religion, and I had no clue who God and the devil were. But we were a happy country family. Life was hunting and fishing, *Leave It to Beaver* and *Andy Griffith*—and a strong work ethic, family togetherness, old-fashioned truthfulness, and a your-handshake-is-your-bond mentality. Dad loved me. I knew he did, but dads of his era just didn't say it much out loud.

But even though my parents weren't religious, Mom sensed religion would be good for me. So she asked our Baptist neighbors down the road if they'd take me to church. Dad (whose name is also Jim) had attended a Lutheran church before I was born—unless it was hunting or fishing season.

One Sunday morning the pastor met my mom at the church door. "Where's Jim?" he asked snidely. "Hunting or fishing again?"

Well, that was that. I think that was the last time either of them darkened the door of any church for a long time.

Back on my bed, my mind reeling from the dream and then the Voice, I found that I'd been jolted to my very soul. But I was also stubborn. The next day I smoked another joint and got high again, and the next day, and the next. But the Voice was stubborn too. Every time I got high it would slice through my fantasies and sober me up: *"Jim. You have a short time to decide."*

"Who are you?" I wondered. "Am I going crazy?"

Chapter 2:

Life's Transition

Little by little, the Voice was wearing me down. And pretty soon, It wasn't the only one talking. I was talking to myself.

Jim, I admitted, *you have royally screwed up your life.*

And I had. Since I wasn't raised in the lap of luxury, Dad and Mom—through their example just as much as their words—let me know that if I wanted anything I was going to have to hit the ground working.

So as a grade-school kid I went around to the neighbors and got as many jobs as I could. I mowed lawns, cleaned houses, raked yards, stacked wood—anything for a buck. And if that sounds wholesome and all-American, think again. It's good to be hard-working and industrious, but in my case I was simply becoming a believer in the idea that money can buy happiness. I guess you could say that money was my first addiction. I even bought huge bags of marbles, rebagged them in smaller bags, and sold them to my classmates.

At age 11 (!) I landed a great little part-time job with Pepsi-Cola Bottling Company. Those were the days before child-labor laws were strictly enforced, and Pepsi let me work as often as I liked—and they paid me well. I sorted cartons, cleaned up broken glass, and did everything and more that was asked of me. To my money addiction I added two more: work and soft drinks. Believe it or not, by the time I was in high school I was glugging down *two six-packs of Pepsi a day*, and when the company merged with a beer and wine distributor I added another addiction: booze. I was on my way to becoming a borderline alcoholic.

By the time I was 15 I worked five hours a day at Pepsi, clogging my system with sugar and ruining it with alcohol. Surprisingly, I was a high school honor roll student. And when I—finally!—reached driving age I sank my Pepsi wages into a red Oldsmobile Cutlass, aluminum engine, dual white racing stripes over the top, custom racing wheels, Hurst four-speed tranny, black leather tuck-and-roll interior, and . . . well, you get the picture. It was a true 60s muscle car. Money was my god.

Before you start thinking that my parents should be taken out and shot for letting me work this much, I assure you that they tried to get me to slow down. But just think of who they were. Dad worked two jobs to keep us financially OK, and Mom was the definition of perpetual motion. I'm exaggerating—but not by much—when I say that every time someone flicked a cigarette ash into an ashtray, she jumped up to clean the tray. So you might say that keeping busy was in my genetic code.

By now I'd stopped going to church unless I happened to be dating a cute girl who was the churchgoing type. Not only did I have no religious leanings, I took great satisfaction in taunting a classmate who talked about his faith in God, ridiculing what would one day provide me my greatest joy.

And as my senior year came to a close, even though I had a wonderful job, lots of money, all the booze I wanted, a fast car, a girlfriend, and the promise of graduating with honors—*and* a job lined up with the local vet to prepare me for a veterinary career—I was starting to test my freedom.

Test. An interesting word, right? "Test" meant drinking and partying more, in spite of my parents' warnings. But at a time in my life when I should have been extremely happy, I wasn't. Something was missing, but I had no idea what it was.

And then came the drugs.

Want to know how I got hooked? You don't have to look any further than an ancient, cool garden.

Hello, Eve. How are you today?

"Hello? Who's that talking? I can't see anybody."

Over here.

"But—"

Yes, that's right. Me. I'm a snake, and I'm talking to you.

"But I thought that snakes can't—"

Look at this.

"Your voice is—lovely."

Look at this.

"Look at what?"

This fruit, you silly girl. It's beautiful, isn't it?

"Y-yes. It is."

I know what you're thinking. God told you not to eat this fruit, right?

"Yes, He did."

There must be some mistake. Are you sure that's what He said?

"I think so."

Sweetheart, this fruit's going to make you wiser than you ever thought you could be. And on top of that, it will give you an experience that's almost unexplainable. Go ahead. Try it.

"But—"

It's only a piece of fruit. It can't hurt you.

Too late, Earth Mother. You've lingered too long, and now you can't resist the urge that's been growing silently within you. Your mind is dancing with your strange new friend's suggestions and you're ignoring every bit of guidance God gave you. Your hand is reaching out, and the smooth, alluring fruit is in your grasp. And now juice is dripping from your lips and cascading down your chin. Your senses are exploding! Every fiber of your being tingles with new awareness.

That's how it feels to take drugs. *That's* the sensation I wanted to share with other kids after I was hooked.

Try it, the devil still says today, about drugs and every other kind of sin. *It'll make you feel wonderful. You'll be elevated to a higher plane of existence. You will experience things you've never experienced before. Go ahead, try it. Just this once.*

"But God says not to," I say feebly.

God's a liar, he hisses contemptuously.

You see, if sin didn't have some "good" points to start with, no one would want to try it. God designed you to be able to feel thrilled, elated, excited. Satan plays off that—but it's only after sin has you in its grasp that you get the downside. The moment Adam and Eve chose to disobey their Lord, it was as though a wicked butcher knife carved a gaping chunk out of them—and that chunk was God, their Life-giver!

And ever since that day, men and women have wandered back and forth across this world trying to satisfy that God-hunger, trying to fill the hole that was created the day they removed their Creator by the exercise of free will.

"Jim," the police chief said to me in the high school principal's office, "you know why you're in here. Right?"

I waited.

"One of the teachers noticed you acting funny, and called me. She thinks you were drinking at lunch today. Blow your breath at me."

I obediently turned my face in his direction, but sucked in rather than blew out. I don't know whether he caught any fumes or not, but his mind was made up.

The principle entered the conversation. "Do you know what this means, Jim?"

"I can't graduate?"

"You'll get your diploma. But you can't take part in any senior activities."

"Not the party?"

"Not the senior party, no."

"And the trip?" I'd been looking forward to the senior trip pretty much all my life. At least that's what it seemed like.

The principal shook his head. "You can't go on the senior trip either."

And if that was a bombshell, another one was waiting for me at home.

"Jim," my dad said grimly, "you're going to junior college this fall. Right here in town."

"But Dad, I want to go to San Jose State!"

"Nope. You're staying here. Looks like we can't trust you out on your own yet."

It wasn't long before I decided it was time to try marijuana. But as a small-town kid I had no idea where to buy it. My town was so "country" and conservative that its people could have written Merle Haggard's hit song for him. You may remember the one that started,

"We don't smoke marijuana in Muskogee. . . "

Maybe we *were* like the Okies from Muskogee. But I learned a soul-rotting truth: no matter how sheltered your life may be, when you set your mind to taste the fruit of the forbidden tree, the devil will always send a helper who guides you to it like a hound dog on the trail of a dirty ol' raccoon.

My hound dog was an old high school friend who showed up one day from San Francisco—and sure enough, he had some grass with him. Not lawn grass, you understand. And after the first few puffs of his marijuana, I knew I wanted more. Amid the buzz, I felt like I was reaching a higher level of thought and existence.

But I was still a hard worker. So much so that at the beginning of the fall college semester I was elected freshman class president, and became active in student government, traveling all over the state to speak on behalf of our school.

Funny thing was, even though I loved speaking to crowds, I got scared to death each time I did.

Guess what came to my rescue.

"Jim Ayer?" The voice on the phone was a Rotary Club member. "A number of us are impressed with how involved your college is in statewide student government. We'd like you to come and speak to us about it."

"Sure," I said. Yet the closer the day came, the sicker I got with stage fright. So the morning of the Rotary meeting I filched one of Mom's tranquilizers from the medicine cabinet. Two hours before I had to leave, it still hadn't kicked in. I took another, and then a third.

When it was my turn to speak, I did so with decorum—I think. But when

I said my last word and floated back to my table, I felt like my Olds Cutlass with a battery charge so low it could barely turn the engine over. It was all my lips could do to form each syllable in order to keep up with the table chitchat. To this day I don't know how I got out of there under my own power, but I later heard that the Rotarians had liked my talk.

And drugs had got me through it.

And since these were the 1960s, that magical decade of liberation—I hope you're detecting the heavy irony in my tone—I wasn't the only one who was discovering what drugs could do.

In 1960 Timothy Leary had traveled to Cuernavaca, Mexico, where he tried some psilocybin mushroom, which is a mind-altering drug. Later he would say that he learned more about psychology in the five hours after taking the drug than he'd learned in his previous 15 years of research. However, I think he'd simply been handed a page from the satanic playbook by the devil himself. I can imagine Eve and Adam, just after they'd eaten the fruit, saying the same thing about their new "knowledge."

So I began listening to Timothy Leary. Drugs, he said, and especially LSD, are the ultimate way to god (he used a small "g"). He would soon coin the phrase, "Turn on, tune in, drop out."

Hmmm, I thought. *The ultimate way to find god.*

I had to admit—even though it was years before I would hear the Voice—that something had been calling out to me. I remember twin girls, Christians, who befriended me and invited me to dinner several times. They co-led a Christian youth group, and always urged me to stay after their nice meal to hear testimonies of changed lives. So most of the time I'd stay. After all, I'd eaten their food. And the meetings were pleasant, with good guitar music. But I continued to block out the calling of the Lord.

Was there a god out there somewhere? Maybe what Leary said was true. Maybe I could find god by allowing drugs to alter my mind.

The school year's almost over, I told myself. *I'm moving to the Bay Area and getting my own apartment. I want to be free—free from parents, from restrictions, from everybody who knows me. I want to be free to roam the big city and do just as I please.* And taking LSD was at the top of my list!

Please. Indulge me in one more quick side comment before I hurry back to my story. This is vital.

It doesn't matter who you are or where you're from, the devil knows how to trap you. I don't know if you've read Doug Batchelor's story, but he was raised in the big city in a billionaire's family, a family which he'll tell you himself was pretty dysfunctional. When he got a chance, he quit school and headed for a cave in Southern California's hills.

I, on the other hand, was raised in the country by a very nonwealthy family, one which was loving and functional and supportive. Good grades came easily to me. And while Doug fled the city for his cave, I fled my small town for the big city. I craved it. I couldn't wait to get there.

So what's the point? *No matter where we're born or whom we're born to, we're all driven by the same "God-hunger." Doug was driven by his emptiness, I was driven by mine. And maybe you're driven by yours.*

Once I got settled into my little Bay Area apartment, I immediately hopped into my car (by this time a hot little '66 Mustang) and roared back toward the country for deer hunting season. It was dusk, and almost impossible to see oncoming cars. Everyone on that two-lane highway had their lights on and was driving cautiously.

Everyone but me.

I'd been behind an 18-wheeler for a long time, and finally nosed the Mustang to the left to get a peek around it to see if I had room to pass.

The coast seemed clear. *Here we go!* In an instant, I was halfway around the semi, going 80, when a tiny gray Volkswagen—with no lights!—appeared directly in front of me, coming my way.

CHAPTER 3:

EASY RIDER—BUT LOST

I had only a heartbeat to react.

To my right loomed the huge truck tires. To my left was a drop-off, which I would later learn was a 20-foot vertical drop-off. When I was almost bumper-to-bumper with the VW, I gave the wheel a hard left yank.

Time seemed to stand still. I left the road and sailed off the embankment, surprisingly flat and straight like a stunt car in an action-movie chase scene. The next instant the Mustang—still traveling fast—slammed down on all four wheels onto a flat grass-covered area between the road bank and a large fenced pasture.

I slowed the car down, and finally came to a stop where the grass had ascended so it was almost even with the highway. Legs trembling, I climbed out and was starting to check the Mustang for damage when I saw that cars, scattered all over the road, had stopped and people were getting out and looking down at me. After checking out the car, I hopped back in, hit the gas, dug dirt, spun mud, clawed my way back onto the road, and took off, leaving everyone standing in amazement across both lanes of traffic. From then on, the Mustang drove down the road with a little bit of a cant, as though to remind me of just how close I had come to death.

A few days later on my hunting trip I killed a deer, a trophy buck. After skinning it, I tossed it into the Mustang. I headed back to the Bay Area, dragged the deer past the swimming pool and into my apartment, and cut the meat into strips which I hung on strings I'd crisscrossed from wall to wall—and then turned the heat up to 90 degrees so it would dry into jerky faster! The bones, of course, I just put in the trash.

Ahhh, city life!

For me and many others my age in that dramatic decade, there was only *one* city—San Francisco. I lived just across the Bay, so it was an easy commute to catch the psychedelic rock groups playing in Winterland or the Fillmore

Auditorium, groups like Jefferson Airplane, Jim Morrison and the Doors, Cream, Jimi Hendrix, and my favorite band, Big Brother and the Holding Company, with lead singer Janis Joplin.

Weekends found me "loaded" (with drugs) and sitting or sprawling with a thousand other "flower children" in the same condition on the floor of the auditorium. Every wild musical chord or drum-roll bent my mind, and every long guitar-riff turned my head inside out. The volume was turned way up, too loud for me to think about the music. The sound simply took me captive, disengaged my brain's "reasoner" (the frontal lobe) and went directly to the pleasure center. To this day when I hear music with a strong beat (on the radio, or even in church!), it beckons to me. It dangles the forbidden fruit before me, and calls me to once again taste the old thrill of acid rock.

What happened to several of my 60s music idols gives a much less glamorous picture of their lives. Jimi Hendrix drowned in his own red-wine vomit in London at the age of 28. Janis Joplin died in a hotel room of a heroin-and-alcohol overdose at 27. The Doors' lead singer Jim Morrison was also 27 when his life snuffed out in a Paris bathtub. There are several theories about why he died, but most of them center on drugs.

Did these people fill their hunger? Did they find their dreams?

Of course not. Real dreams aren't found in drugs. Or in music.

"Jim."

I was so loaded I found it hard to drive a car on northbound Interstate 5 and talk to my friend at the same time.

"Jim!"

"What?"

"Why you pulling over, man?"

I guided the Mustang to the edge of the freeway and turned off the engine. It was night.

"Get out," I said.

"Why, man?"

"Just get out. You and me both."

He slid from his seat and I slid from mine. "OK, do what I do," I said. Captivated by the darkness of night, I drifted to the center of one of the freeway lanes and lay down.

"Whatcha doin'?"

"Look, look," I said. "This is far out. I'm watching for cars. The road stretches to eternity."

"Far out, you say? That isn't cool, man! I ain't doin' that."

"Oh yeah, you've gotta try this."

He paused, then finally crawled over and flopped down beside me. "Oh man, you were right! This is awesome!"

And nobody who's ever travelled that busy stretch of freeway is going to believe me, but my buddy and I must have lain for 15 minutes on the cold concrete of the main north-south freeway from Canada to Mexico, and not one single car came along! Miles to the south, God—for reasons of His own—must have drastically thinned out that traffic.

But don't push your luck. Never assume that God will always watch over you no matter what you do. I had friends and other people I knew that are dead, because actions have consequences. A drunk classmate of mine, riding his Harley, came over a hill and smashed straight into an oncoming car. Another "loaded" friend tried to kill himself by putting a shotgun (also loaded) to his stomach and pulling the trigger. He survived, but he's never been the same.

Because when God sees we're continually ignoring His tender calls of mercy, and when our cosmic cup of wrong choices is full to the brim . . . with great hesitation He finally withdraws His voice of longing, and His protection along with it, and allows the devil to sweep us into oblivion.

Moving to Oakland a bit later, I lived in a boarding house in a really tough neighborhood where a radical group called the Black Panthers fought gun battles with the police. I got a job at the American Can Company, but the same drugs which killed my desire for college were also murdering my work ethic. So I drew a paycheck only long enough to buy a 650 BSA motorcycle—a pretty nice bike in those days.

I'd ridden motorcycles for years, and already had many wrecks and broken bones. My first crash was at age 15. A car and house trailer broadsided me in an intersection, crushing my ankle. My next close call was a concussion, and a broken leg and nose, at age 17. Now it was time to play *Easy Rider* (a popular motorcycle movie at the time). Dennis Hopper and Peter Fonda had nothing on me. I was cool. I welded a big "sissy bar" to the back of the bike, roped my sleeping bag to it, and headed for New York.

That is, after a slight delay. I was arrested and thrown in jail for shoplifting. Even though I had $160 in my wallet, I stole a chocolate candy bar.

Once I'd paid my debt to society, I studied my clothes. "This isn't an 'outlaw biker' outfit!" I snorted. "I've got to improve my wardrobe." So I bought a Levi jeans-jacket and cut off the sleeves. So far, so good, but I still wouldn't be able to mix among the Hell's Angels. I took my new jacket out to a truck parking lot which had a lot of dirt and old grease. Tossing it down, I started grinding it into the pavement with my boot. "That's more like it," I chuckled happily. "Grease, dirt—and smell!"

The handsome country boy, the honor student, the solidly dependable worker, the ethical and honest young man with a promising future, had all but disappeared. I was now a lying, stealing, smelly motorcycle scumbag who once in a while even carried a gun and a knife.

And I was still dealing drugs. I used every bit of finesse and salesmanship I knew to turn people on to drugs. It literally became my goal to have everyone I met experience marijuana and LSD—and money wasn't my main motivation. I'd simply bought into the culture that Timothy Leary had been preaching. I wanted everyone to feel the "ecstasy." To my great regret, I experienced a high success rate. I'd become a dedicated evangelist for the great deceiver.

And if I came across someone whose morals and ethics kept them from trying drugs, I took on the challenge of converting them, and was often successful. Because unless your morals and standards are planted solidly on the saving power of God and the protection of the Holy Spirit, you're like a ship without an anchor. The deceiver will always send someone your direction to speak enticing words that offer happiness, joy, peace, and a new and exciting experience.

As a former "druggie evangelist" I can tell you that if you'd come to me with only a few weak reasons for not taking drugs, I probably would have converted you. You see, I believed what I believed more fanatically than most half-hearted Christians believed what they believed. They were no match for me.

There are still moments in my life when my mind races back across the years of sin, not with longing but with deep regret. All the time and energy spent doing evil causes me great pain. But then my Lord puts His arms around me and says, "I have put your sins behind My back, I have cast them into the depths of the sea; you need to do the same." Remorse for sin and its consequences is good—it shows that the Lord can make our consciences tender again—but our focus should always be upward and onward. Praise God for His mercy and love!

But astride my motorcycle, rumbling in the direction of New York, I felt no guilt. In fact, since for some weird reason I had routed the first leg of my journey through the Mojave Desert—in summertime!—I felt nothing but the 120-degree heat. Back then there weren't a lot of stopping places, but every time I found a watering hole I soaked my bandana, my shirt, and my body from head to toe with water, then headed east again.

And straight into a roadblock set up by a loving God.

Chapter 4:

Uncomfortable Encounters

Not a *real* highway roadblock, of course.

If God would have had a road crew string yellow-and-black-striped barriers across the highway, I would have simply hit the ditch and bounced through fields until I found a usable travel surface again. Instead, I believe God used the motorcycle itself to turn me around.

That high-quality, normally dependable 650 BSA died on me four miles outside of Needles, California. I knew that Needles was a dust-hole in the middle of a burning desert. I knew it had a tiny population and I had no hope of anyone with skills or parts to fix my bike. But Needles was the closest town, and even though I was stranded with no water and lots of sun, I didn't want to leave the bike by itself. So I began to push that heavy hunk of metal down the road.

A mile or so later a truck rolled up beside me.

"Hey, there," a gruff voice said. "I hear you need some help."

It turned out that my Good Samaritan was—get this—an old biker. Together we hoisted the bike onto his truck bed, and drove to his house. This guy had an entire graveyard of old bikes, pieces, and parts lying or stacked everywhere! And after some good wrench work and "new" parts, I was, as the band Steppenwolf sang, "Headin' on the high road, lookin' for adventure."

I made it to Kingman, Arizona, before the next breakdown happened. Some wonderful people at a local cycle shop had me back on the road in no time. I repaid them by stealing a motorcycle helmet when they weren't looking.

By Flagstaff I'd ruined my clutch cable, and found that Phoenix was the only place to get a new one. That meant I had to ride more than 100 miles, over varied terrain, shifting without using my clutch. Not quite the '*Easy Rider*' adventure I was hoping for.

"But I'm not giving up!" I growled as the bike and I lurched into Phoenix.

For some reason—and I do believe that maybe a Divine Hand was working to keep me out West—I headed not east but north to Salt Lake City, and from there to Jackson Hole, Wyoming, where I got a job at a local restaurant. Suddenly amidst all those country hicks I was the cool biker guy from San Francisco, and I became a leader among the local rabble. Nights, we hung out in the town park where, at one point, I scrambled to the top of a huge boulder with a can of hairspray. While tourists stood open-mouthed, I pressed the button and held a lighted match to the spraying mist. And as this flaming torch pierced the dark night sky, I screamed, "I am the god of hellfire!"

The local police force were deeply suspicious of this new California biker, especially after they caught wind that I was dealing drugs. These were the days before Miranda rights and sensitivity to police brutality, so one day these cowboy cops simply loaded me and a few other guys into a truck, drove us over the Montana border in the middle of the night, and dumped us off. "And don't come back!" they shouted as they roared away.

Well, I *had* to get back, because my bike was still in Jackson Hole. As soon as I hit town again I got word that the cops were going to arrest me on drug charges. Luckily my bike was running, so I got my stuff together and headed for the wilds of the Teton Mountains until a friend found someone who could sneak me out of the state. We loaded my bike into a panel truck and headed, not toward New York, but back to my California hometown of Mount Shasta.

But I'm not telling Mom and Dad, I decided.

A few friends and I rented a little ranch house, and we cooked one of our first meals in a large cooking pot I'd found buried in the yard. "We don't owe society anything. Society owes *us*" was our motto, so we didn't pay much attention to law and order. What we needed—or wanted—we took. We shot a deer out of season, hung it up in the nonrefrigerated barn, and cut slabs off it when we got hungry. To this day I'm not sure why we didn't die of food poisoning.

One day, heading toward the local college to meet friends and sell some drugs, I saw my mom's car coming in the opposite direction.

Oh, no, I thought. *What am I going to say? Do I have time to—*

Too late. She'd spotted me.

Pulling to the side of the road, I rolled down my window. "Hi, Mom."

"Honey! You're back in town!"

"Yeah, I've been back for a little while." I paused. "I was going to let you know."

She was surprised to see me, but she'd heard from friends that I was back in the area, so she'd been keeping a hopeful eye out for me or my car.

"How are you doing?" she asked, and I could hear a mother's heartbroken love in her voice.

"I'm OK," I said uncomfortably, "but I've got get going."

We talked for another minute or two and then I drove off. I could tell that I was breaking her heart. *But my freedom's more important,* I told myself.

Mom and Dad and I were playing out the separation scenario. Like all parents, they'd brought their own problems into our family unit, because they'd been shaped by their families while growing up. Now I'd made choices of my own, and brought these into the family as well. All of us are living in a mix of inherited and self-created problems, and the only way to climb out of them is with God's help. The only way to grow a circle of love is with Him in the middle, holding everyone close. God's plan is the only one that works, and He's always there to help you work past the hurt and misunderstandings—and even the hate, if it exists. If you let Him, He'll wrap His mighty arms gently around you and hold you ever so tenderly, offering comfort, healing, and new life.

After my reunion chat with Mom I headed back to my rented farmhouse, and opened the secret location where I hid my drugs.

"Hey!" I said aloud. "Some of my stuff is missing."

I counted again and again, and when I was sure, I confronted one of my housemates.

"Did you take some of my stuff?" I asked him.

Finally he admitted that he had. I was upset about the loss of the drugs, but even more upset that the old saying about "honor among thieves" wasn't true after all.

Now, of course, I'm not surprised. It's like the old story about the turtle and the scorpion. The turtle crawls to the edge of the river, and is about to step in when he hears a scorpion's voice.

"I need to get to the other side," the scorpion says. "Can I hitch a ride on your back?"

"No way," says the turtle. "You're going to wait until my neck is exposed, and you're going to sting me, and I'll die."

"Are you crazy?" the scorpion asked. "If I sting you out there in the river we'll both drown. All I want is to get across."

"That makes sense," the turtle says. "Hop on, then."

The scorpion jumps on his back and away they go. Halfway across the deep river the turtle feels a sharp pain in his neck.

"Hey!" he cries in agony. "What are you doing? Now we're both going to die!"

"Sorry," the scorpion sighs. "I just couldn't help myself. It's my nature."

That's what had happened to me. I'd taken the devil on my back, and now he was slowly killing me. Maybe you too are feeling the sting and the burning of his poison. You need not drown, however, because Jesus has taken the sting for you and suffered all the poison on your behalf.

Disgusted with my housemate's theft, I packed up and moved to another house with another set of roommates. These guys were also heavily into drugs, and most of us got high on a daily basis. This was a much smaller house, and I was forced to spend much of my time in my bedroom, which seemed only slightly larger than a postage stamp.

And that was when, sitting on the edge of my unmade bed one morning, high on marijuana, the floor fell away from me, and from a high perch in stadium bleachers, I watched God and the devil discuss the fate of my soul.

Then came the Voice: *"Jim. You have a short time to decide."*

And as I mentioned back in chapter 1, the Voice wouldn't let me alone. The next day I smoked another joint and got high again, and the next day, and the next. But the Voice was stubborn too. Every time I got high it would slice through my fantasies and sober me up: *"Jim. You have a short time to decide."*

Decide *what?* What was I supposed to do?

Deep down inside I knew. But since I didn't want to listen, I chose to remain ignorant. But getting high was absolutely no fun with the Voice sounding in my ears.

"This is driving me crazy," I finally decided. "I'm going to quit drugs and move back home." Anyway, the cops were arresting several people I knew for dealing and possession. A different place to stay—rent-free—was what I needed right then. So Mom and Dad gladly took me in.

The downside, of course, was that now I had to take orders from someone else. And I wasn't the only one who felt stress when we all were together again. Remember how my mom was so obsessed by cleanliness that it was all she could do to keep from emptying a cigarette ashtray every time an ash landed in it?

"If I'm going to eat my meals with you," I demanded, "Icarus is going to have a place at the table too." (Icarus was a beagle and Siberian husky cross I'd picked up after I'd come back from Jackson Hole. I'd named him for the young man in Greek mythology whose father had built him a set of wings made from wax and feathers. He died when he flew too close to the sun.)

Mom's eyes widened. "Your *dog?* At the table? Not in my house!"

"Icarus is part of the family," I said sternly. "*My* family, anyway. He eats with us, and he's got to have his own chair."

Mom and Dad got used to Icarus eventually. One day they went on an errand, leaving their Chihuahua and Icarus together in the house. When they got back home they saw blood spattered everywhere. Horrified, they immediately assumed that Icarus had devoured the tiny dog. But both were fine—the Chihuahua had bitten Icarus' ear!

Later I actually let Icarus join me on dates. He took a dislike to one young college girl and urinated all over her in the car. I apologetically drove her to her dorm, where she changed into new things. Once back in the car, Icarus proceeded to defecate on her!

Though I'd moved back home, I still wanted my independence. In addition to insisting that Icarus join us for meals, I waited until a day both Mom and Dad were gone, then tore my bed frame apart and flopped my mattress onto the floor. I hauled in my cruddy old drug table, and I unrolled my beat-up rug and arranged it beside the mattress.

Ahhhhhh, I sighed. *Now that's the hippie look.*

My poor mother, who loved me so much, said very little when she opened the door and saw my transformed room.

As the days passed, I actually tried to read the Bible, searching for some anchor point or direction. But even though I had stopped using drugs for the time being, my thinking was still clouded, and I couldn't seem to grasp the meaning of the Scriptures. Weeks tumbled into months, but my mind still hungered for a "trip," that momentary transport to nonreality.

Chapter 5:

Jungle Jim's

Once I'd stopped uploading drugs into my mind, their effects began to subside, and I found that some of my old ambition was coming back.

I used to want to be a veterinarian, I thought. *But the last thing I want is to go back to school. Hey—maybe I should open a pet shop! That'll let me be close to the animals I love.*

My parents were delighted to see that I now had a direction in life.

"Jim," they said, "if you're really serious about this, we'd be happy to give you the money we've been setting aside for your education."

I also cashed out an insurance policy I'd purchased several years before, and with all this capital in hand, I was ready for my new adventure. My first task was to travel to bigger cities and talk to pet supply wholesalers and animal importers. They were very skeptical.

"You want to open a pet shop in *Mount Shasta?*"

"Sure."

"You'll never make it."

"How come?"

"Your population base is too small."

Whoa there, I thought. *Don't ever say, "You can't do it" to Jim Ayer. That's like a matador waving a red cape in front of a bull—it's my signal to charge ahead. You just watch and see.*

First I rented what would become the perfect store, and built shelves and stocked them with pet supplies. Then I constructed animal cages and installed aquariums. As I worked, I wondered, *What shall I call my new enterprise?*

One day I had lunch with the veterinarian I'd previously worked for. After we finished eating, we walked by my store.

"What are you going to name it?" he asked.

"I don't know."

"Since your name is Jim, you should call it 'Jungle Jim's.'"

And soon Jungle Jim's was known for buying, training, and selling exotic animals across the entire western United States. To this day I meet adults who tell me how excited they were to visit my store when they were kids. "It was like going to the zoo!" they say.

It was fun for me, too. Because when I say exotic animals, I'm not talking about the pink rabbits you find in the mall on Easter Sunday. No, I sold wolves and cougars (pen-raised and bottle-fed). I imported parrots, macaws, vultures, hawks, and owls. Some of my favorite friends were the monkeys, especially the big spider monkeys and gibbon apes. I usually had one running around—or should I say *hanging* around.

I sold Malayan sun bears, bobcats, and jungle cats—even an African lion. People who walked through our store saw animals they'd never even heard of, such as agoutis, grisons, capybaras, Asian otters, and a large variety of snakes. BIG snakes. Ask me what was the biggest snake I ever sold.

"Jim, what was the biggest snake you ever sold?"

I'm so glad you asked! If I remember right, it was a 12-foot anaconda. In person, and up close, a 12-foot anaconda is *very, very* big!

Looking back, I can't believe that during those first few years of owning Jungle Jim's, I was still a proud evolutionist. Since then, of course, I've learned that the animal kingdom is one of the windows into the personality of God—a window smeared and darkened by sin, but still a window. How can you watch the antics of a monkey and not believe that the Creator has not only a sense of humor but also a love for all His creation? And when a spider monkey wraps his arms affectionately around your neck, snuggles his head against your cheek, and softly talks to you—yes, I did say "talks"—how could you not suspect the existence of an "In-the-beginning God"?

But my mind hadn't started running in those channels yet. And anyway, I had my hands—and my brain—full with running a fun and adventurous business. You just never knew what would happen in an exotic-pet store.

One day I was chatting with a couple that had stopped by to see my animals and to talk. The conversation went on for several minutes and as I relaxed, I leaned back against one of the animal cages. A split second later a rush of pain shot from my rear end all the way up my spine. *There's a capybara in the cage behind you!* the pain shouted. *It has just sunk its inch-long teeth through your pants and into your rump!*

This presented a problem. If I'd been an ordinary civilian I could have screamed bloody murder and called for first aid. But Jungle Jim could not lose his composure in front of potential clients.

Still holding on to what I hope was a pleasant smile, I considered the situation. *Aha,* I thought, remembering whose cage I'd leaned against. *What's caus-*

ing me to experience this excruciating pain is the world's biggest rodent. It has bad breath and foul teeth. What do I do now?

Fortunately the capybara had released me, probably deciding that this bit of "rare" human steak needed a little Heinz 57 sauce. I glided gracefully sideways away from his cage, and casually placed one hand behind my back. Probing gently, I discovered that my pants were now very damp—with my blood.

"Are there any other questions I can answer for you?" I murmured, and then decided that this was no time for idle chitchat. "Uh . . . if you'll excuse me for a moment, I need to check on something."

Keeping my backside away from public view, I limped to the restroom. Sure enough, that was my own precious blood I had felt. I quickly added another "staff rule" to the Jungle Jim operating policy. Staff rule 1 was never to scream or cause panic in the store—no matter what. Staff rule 2: never back up to a cage containing an animal with teeth large enough to reach through the bars and impale your body!

Speaking of teeth, we had a beautiful male bobcat named Shiloh. Mom and Dad had taken him home with them from time to time, and absolutely loved him. Mom was the Jungle Jim bookkeeper, dog groomer, and all-round great helper. She loved to play with the animals and help customers between grooming appointments.

On one particular day, which historians will no doubt later speak of as "the Battle of Shiloh," Jungle Jim's was full of people. Mom was having a wonderful time playing with Shiloh. Her friend Carol had stopped in to visit and was somewhere else in the store.

Suddenly Shiloh sunk his teeth deep into Mom's arm, and kept them there.

Still smiling, my intrepid mother got a grip on Shiloh's upper jaw and tried to work it loose. It wouldn't come.

"Carol?" Mom called brightly. "*Carol?* Could you please come here for a second and help me?"

Carol appeared, but as soon as she saw what was happening, she shrank back in fear—and Mom was on her own. Grasping Shiloh's jaws again, she twisted and pried and finally got his mouth open.

Smiling graciously at the watching customers, Mom approached me. "That cat bit me," she whispered, barely moving her lips. "I'm going to the ER." The puncture wounds were large, but she compressed the bleeding area with her hand, and quietly left the store in search of stitches and antibiotics. She was back a couple of hours later to finish the day's dog grooming!

Another time Mom was talking with a female customer.

"Do you have any suggestions," the woman asked her, "about what type of pet might make a good companion for my son?"

"Have you thought of a gecko?" Mom asked. "Let me show you one." She reached into a cage. As her index finger approached the gecko's head, he made a grunting noise, then executed a rapid, precise move that snipped off the small, fleshy part of Mom's finger.

Remembering Jungle Jim's staff rule 1, Mom calmly pinched the end of her blood-pouring finger and finished the conversation with the shocked customer. Not surprisingly, the woman quickly backed away. "I . . . I don't think I'll buy one of those," she said, and hurried out.

"Mom," I told her with a grin, "You just lost me a sale."

Want to know where I got any grit and tenacity I may possess? You've just met her.

Just one more Jungle Jim story. I've told you about the Battle of Shiloh, and now I'll tell you about World War III.

Caring for pet store animals is hard, seven-days-a-week work. Other stores open their doors at 9:00 a.m. and are ready for business, but my store had animals that did their business all night long. This meant that we had a huge amount of cleanup to do every morning.

First thing every morning we'd open both the front and back doors to allow the cool morning air to circulate through the store. Then we started feeding the animals and cleaning their cages, hoping to get everything ready by opening time. Akita, my pet Siberian husky who accompanied me to work, watched with interest.

Among our guests at that point was a pair of squirrel monkeys. Don't tell them I said so, but in my professional opinion squirrel monkeys are the worst kind for human companionship. Not only are they flighty and high-strung, but they don't normally form close relationships with people.

My unsuspecting mother unfastened the lock on the squirrel cage, and cracked open the door just wide enough to clean out the papers and place fresh food in their dish.

"Oh, *no!*" she screamed.

Back when I was a kid there was a cartoon called "Mighty Mouse" about a superhero rodent. These squirrel monkeys must have been regular watchers, because one of them leaped against the cage door and gave it a quick shove. The other shot through the door and scrambled across Mom's head. On his way to freedom he managed to hook her wig, rip it from its underpinnings, and leave it dangling from her head. The first squirrel (Mighty Mouse) followed.

"They're out!" Mom screamed. "They're out!"

I raced for the open doors, and slammed first one and then the other, just in time.

Grinning with delight, Akita the Siberian husky sprang into action, chasing after the monkeys. This panicked the dynamic duo and they fled wildly across the shelves.

"Where's the animal net?" I shouted.

"Over there!" Mom replied.

I grabbed the net and soon was in hot pursuit. "Gotcha! Whoops, I *almost* had him!"

"There they go!" called Mom, like a racetrack announcer.

Try to imagine the scene—two tiny demons skittering at breakneck speed across our well-stocked shelves, pushing the supplies over the edge and onto the floor. One shelf, two shelves, three, and rapidly four, fell victim to the chase. I dashed around a corner in a swift move to try to net the perpetrators, and snagged my shirt on a well-placed hook, tearing a gaping hole.

Mom spotted a chance to catch them, and lunged forward—and fell, tearing her nylons from top to bottom. *"Oooff,"* she said. Shelves 5 through 10 succumbed to the scourge of the escaping pair. Now the floor was almost impassable because of the piles of canned goods, cat toys, fish supplies, and who knows what else.

"We've gotta catch those guys!" I shouted. "Time's running out!"

So Jungle Jim mustered all of his stalking ability and, aided by his trusty dog, finally cornered one of the escapees and ended its rampage. Now all that was left was number 2.

"There he goes!" Mom cried, and sure enough, the corner of my eye caught the motion of the desperate monkey. I leaped toward him, but missed. He scampered across shelves 11 through 13, heaving supplies in my direction as he went. I tore my pant leg.

Finally the tiny menace made a mistake, and I grabbed him. As the proverbial dust settled, Mom and I stood in the middle of our war zone staring at one another. I spoke first.

"You oughtta see what you look like," I giggled as I surveyed Mom's wig dangling from her unkempt hair, her disheveled shirt, and her ripped nylons.

"Go look in the mirror yourself," she retorted, and burst into laughter. Curious, I found a mirror and gazed into it. The mighty Jungle Jim's shirt was ripped far beyond repair, his shirttails were dangling, his pant leg displayed a gaping hole, and he was perspiring profusely, hair hanging across his flushed face.

Then we both turned to survey the damage. Pandemonium stretched from wall to wall, all the way to the entrance.

"Uh-oh," I gulped. "Customers at the door!"

Maybe in heaven, sitting in a happy meadow among all sorts of animals, I can tell you some more of my Jungle Jim stories. Like the wallaby who hopped out of her cage one morning, but was cornered in the bathroom by Akita. Or the macaw who flew out the front door and over the rooftops, finally coming to rest in a treetop where I had to climb up and get her.

Or the poodle who'd just had a bath and was under the hair dryer, but slipped her collar, jumped off the grooming table, and ran out the door as fast as her freshly-groomed pom-pom feet would carry her. I'm sure we presented quite a sight running down the center of Main Street—poodle in the lead and me in hot pursuit. The chase ended a half-mile later in a black-mud drainage ditch. Now it was shampoo time for us *both*!

Or the five-foot boa constrictor I sold to a family. Delighted with him, they'd wrap him under their shirt and take him shopping. One day they lost him in a Safeway supermarket. Not only did they not find him, they never told the store manager! I never read about a lawsuit, so I assume no one found him in the produce section.

Chapter 6:

Companionship

"Have gun, will travel" reads the card of a man . . .*

The light-bluish glow of the TV set illuminated a circle of faces in my parents' living room. Dad's eyes were glued to the screen, as they always were when his favorite program, the Western cowboy serial *Have Gun—Will Travel,* began with its familiar "Paladin, Paladin" theme song.

Mom sat beside him doing her best to keep an expression of polite interest on her face. Privately, she ranked the weekly adventures of Paladin, gunfighter and champion of justice, slightly below the level of interest she displayed toward the home life of the common earthworm. *But tonight is special,* she told herself. *We've got to make a good impression on Jim's girlfriend, Janene. And she's a real sweetheart. I can see she's trying to make a good impression on us too.*

Indeed she was, I can confidently say. Beverly Janene Thompson had grown up in a town a few miles away, and was someone I'd known for several years, mainly because I'd dated several of her girlfriends. But now, here she was, pretty and blond, sitting primly on a chair near my mom, eyes dutifully on the screen.

I had coached her well. "There's a little rule of thumb we'll have to observe," I'd told her earlier. "When we're watching *Have Gun—Will Travel,* nobody talks. And especially not at the very end of the program. Dad always looks forward to that final gunfight."

But there was one other thing I'd prepared her for—and which she had totally forgotten.

During the next half-hour we watched Paladin work his way through the crisis of the week with a combination of crisp, forceful comments and an occasional volley of gunshots. And as the final showdown with the bad guys approached, I stole a glance at my father. Sure enough, Jim Ayer, Senior, had that familiar look of intense concentration.

Breaking the no-talk rule, I made a casual comment to Janene in a soft voice.

Janene promptly rose to her feet, stepped gracefully over to the TV, and squarely in the middle of the show's most crucial moment, pushed in the volume knob, turning off the set. Then she walked gracefully back and sat beside me.

Oh, it was a joy to watch my dad's face. For an instant I saw a mix of anger and annoyance, which was quickly replaced by a stare of stunned bewilderment. *Who is this psychotic young lady who has just ruined my program?* his expression said. *And how did she ever become friends with my son?*

I couldn't hold it any longer. I roared with laughter, slapping my knee again and again.

Everyone looked at me, puzzled—and Janene's face was just as puzzled as anyone else. *I must have done something funny, or strange,* she seemed to be thinking. *But what was it?*

"It worked!" I chuckled. "It worked!"

"*What* worked?" asked Mom.

"Hypnotism!" I said. "This morning Janene let me hypnotize her. I told her that when I said a certain key phrase, she must get up and turn off the TV. Then I told her that she would not remember being told to do this. And a minute ago I said the key phrase to her!"

I don't know who laughed first, but soon we were all laughing, even Janene—though what was funniest of all was her puzzled expression.

For me, immersing myself in the mystic realm of hypnotism was just another way of trying to fill the void, the hole in my life. Later, of course, I came to realize that it was simply another tool of the deceiver, who is always at work, doing all in his power to tempt us to surrender our wills to his destructive ways. I'm confident that he uses hypnosis as one more way to control minds.

"But doctors use it all the time," I can hear someone say. I know, but I still stand by what I have said. When you allow anyone to place your mind in neutral—when you instruct the mind's gatekeepers to stand down—you give over control to a lower power.

Meanwhile, I was about to lose my own battle to a lower power. I'd been off drugs for quite awhile, but like many community businesspeople I'd been going to bars and other gatherings where alcohol was served—and putting down my share of it.

One night in a bar I cried out in desperation, "I've got to find some drugs!"

So much for Jungle Jim's drug-free resolution. I was about to learn that promises without the power of God to sustain them are worthless. They're like trying to hold a mighty ship at a dock with ropes made out of sand.

Almost immediately the door of the bar swung open, and in walked a seedy-looking character. The saying "It takes one to know one" came true again that evening. I immediately knew that he was packing drugs—and better yet, he needed a ride to the town where Janene lived.

"I'll give you a lift," I said, and after a few more drinks we were off.

It turns out that my passenger had been doing his own "It takes one to know one" analysis. Almost as soon as the car doors clicked shut he asked, "Want to smoke a joint?"

The rest is history. *And this time I heard no Voice telling me that I had a short time to decide. I could now have fun destroying myself with no outside interference.*

Well, I was back on drugs. And it wasn't long before I suggested to Janene that she experiment with them. I'm going to let Janene herself tell you what happened.

Janene: Much time had passed before I started dating Jim or anyone for that matter. You see, I had been engaged to be married. My fiancé, Jerry, had served in Vietnam. Upon his return home we spent much time planning the grand event. It was going to be a large Catholic wedding. I had a beautiful dress with a long flowing train, several bridesmaids, hundreds of guests, a large reception—all of the big wedding things.

But it ended in tragedy. Around midnight of the morning of our wedding day I received a phone call from my future brother-in-law. He and Jerry had been out partying at a bar and there was an argument—I'm sure it was about the war and the National Guard—and blows were exchanged. Jerry was struck in the chest, causing his heart to fibrillate. He fell backwards and hit his head on the cement. He died, on our wedding morning, on the floor of the bar. He was 22 years old. My life, my future, ended that night.

When Jim first asked me about using marijuana I was not at all interested. I always carefully considered what would happen if I did something wrong and got caught. In school, if someone was going to get caught doing something they shouldn't, it would be me. However Jim kept coming up with one argument after another.

He'd already started hypnotizing me, and you have to work through some trust issues before you can allow someone to have that kind of power over you. I was developing a real trust in him, and I was also truly falling in love. However I didn't want to admit this to myself—much less to him, because I knew he wasn't interested in getting serious.

But Jim was very persuasive, and while I wasn't overly crazy about taking drugs, I did enjoy having fun with him. However, after a while I told him I'd decided I didn't want to get high any more.

Then one Sunday I was at work at the phone company. On my break, I looked out toward the parking lot, and lo and behold, Jim was parked there. So I walked outside and went over to his car.

"Hi," I said. "What are you doing here?"

"Waiting for you."

"How come?"

"I want to talk to you about something."

I glanced doubtfully at my watch. "I don't get off for two more hours."

"I'll wait."

"OK," I said. "I'll try to get off early if I can."

Back in the building, I started pestering my supervisor to let me off early. Finally she said yes, more to get rid of me than anything else.

"Janene," Jim asked me when I was inside the car. "Will you get high with me just one last time?"

I frowned. "Why?"

"Because I want to ask you something, and I want to you to be high with me when I ask you."

Finally I said, "Well, just one more time."

He drove me to a very special place along the Sacramento River. In the distance, gigantic granite cliffs towered high above fragrant evergreens. For awhile we dangled our feet in the cool, cascading stream. We lit up a joint and smoked it for a while, and suddenly Jim turned to me.

"Janene," he said, "will you marry me?"

I wasn't ready for that question. However, I didn't have to think about it very long.

"Yes," I said faintly.

I accepted the proposal with peace and happiness in my heart. I knew that this was a life-changing moment.

Little did I know how just how life-changing it would be.

"Let's make a vow," I said to him. "Let's vow right now that no matter what, we will make our marriage work."

"I'll vow that," he said instantly. "We'll never get a divorce."

"We'll never get a divorce," I repeated. "We will make our marriage work."

"We will make our marriage work," he echoed.

We didn't have a long engagement. We were married two and a half weeks later.

Jim: The only minister I knew was an Episcopalian priest who boarded his very large Burmese cat, Benji, at our animal hospital during his many travels. The pastor was very proud of how tough Benji was, and told me that the cat had attacked a vet in Texas while boarding there. Benji lived up to his reputation, and I always made sure I had a broom and garbage can lid handy every time I moved him from one kennel to the next.

We were married in my parents' backyard. Everyone crowded around the Koi pond to hear us exchange our vows.

Janene: It had taken me a long time to recover from Jerry's death and the fact that he'd died on our wedding day. So when Jim asked me to marry him I didn't want to wait. I wanted it to happen right away. And no big wedding plans this time, or anything that went with it. I wanted only our parents there, and to get married by the pond that Jim had built at the store.

Then Jim's mom graciously offered their home. His parents have always treated me like a daughter and have been so very supportive of me. I love them like my own. I asked my mom to make a very simple white dress for me, and asked a close friend to stand up with me. In the end, about 50 very dear friends and family joined us in a beautiful, simple wedding. As a wedding gift, Jim's aunt and uncle sent us to their cabin at Donner Lake for our honeymoon. We had a great beginning to our new life together. Little did we realize what an adventurous road we were on.

Jim: Now we had an even greater reason to make Jungle Jim's a success—we wanted to provide for some little Jungle Jims! And sure enough, we had a beautiful baby boy. We named him Jason, after the movie *Jason and the Argonauts*.

And suddenly, the Lord invited Himself into our lives.

Invited? That word seems terribly tame for what He really did.

Chapter 7:

Found!

It happened like this.

When you own your own business, as Janene and I did, you're virtually married to it. It would be a long time before we'd have an extended vacation, but we did take a day off from time to time.

One day we bundled up our precious little Jason and drove to Sacramento to see some college friends. I spent most of the day high on drugs with them.

"Janene," I said laughingly as we walked back to the car, "you've got to drive. I'm too loaded."

As soon as we got home I lit up another joint. This time Janene joined me, taking puffs while she was changing baby on the kitchen table. (It was a small house.)

I drifted into the bedroom.

And suddenly the Voice I had not heard for years spoke to me. But this time its message was different.

Jim. Tonight is your last night to decide!

I just stood there, my face numb. I didn't argue. I knew the Voice meant what It said.

"No debate," I mumbled. "No more time. This is it. Tonight I must make my choice." The crossroads of eternity seemed to spread before me. My mind raced. "Which road? Which road shall I take? One will lead to life, the other to death."

How was I so sure that this was an eternal life/eternal death choice? I don't really know. Maybe it was the many encounters I'd had with Christians over the years—the twin sister youth leaders, conversations in a park in Jackson Hole, even discussions I'd had with others while high on drugs. Somehow the seeds had been planted. The harvest was delayed—but finally the crop came in.

OK, I said to myself, *I'll follow the Voice.*

I went to my drug stash, gathered everything up, and headed for the kitchen to tell Janene what had just happened. By the time I got to her, all I said was, "I've got to flush this down the toilet."

Janene looked at me, smiled, and said, "OK, honey." She seemed too stoned to really grasp what I was saying.

Standing over the toilet bowl, I poured everything in and pushed the flush-handle. The moment I heard the gurgle and the rush of water it felt like the weight of the entire world lifted from my shoulders—a weight I hadn't realized I was carrying. But it felt so good, *so good!*

I began to cry, and found myself on my knees, gripping that cool porcelain as tears of relief and joy flowed freely. Amid my sobs, I heard something, and turned to find Janene in the doorway. She was crying too.

Janene: I was so relieved that we were going to be done with this type of life. I loved my husband and son with all my heart, but I was so tired of the drugs. On the night Jason was born, Jim got high and then to tried to put the crib together. He put all of the screws in the wrong holes, so the crib was never quite right. That was how our life had been—never quite right. Now I had hope that things would be right.

Jim: Once my sobs had stopped, I stood to my feet and looked at Janene. "Will you join me in . . . in a prayer?" I asked awkwardly.

"Yes," she said.

Eyes brimming with tears, we walked into the living room and embraced. And I uttered maybe the first—and almost certainly the shortest—prayer I have ever prayed.

"God," I said, "I'm sorry it took so long."

That was it. No fancy phrases, no long recital. Just a few simple words spoken from deep within my heart. I had finally responded to the Voice that had been calling me for so long. And it was God's voice. Of that I had no doubt!

I once was lost but now I'm found, I remember thinking. *What joy, what happiness, what peace.* Actually, I hadn't been lost in the normal sense of the word, because God knew where I was all along. As with Adam and Eve in the garden, the Lord had never taken His eyes off me or Janene. He knew exactly where we were, every moment of every day. And as I wandered far away from Him, He continued to call me to come home.

This means so much to me that I can't go on without asking you something. The reason we're lost is that Adam and Eve passed the "rebellion gene" on to us. We're *born* lost. Our only hope is the same as Adam and Eve's only hope—to respond to the sweet voice of God. He will completely forgive you and restore you to His heavenly family. I hope that you have already answered His call, but if you have not, won't you please do it right now?

Maybe you're like I was, afraid that if you answer, it will cause you to lose out on some benefit. You want to be your own man or woman, so you've ignored the call time and time again. *I urge you not to wait. I can tell you truthfully and without any hesitation that I have never been unhappy because of answering God's voice. The opposite is just so overwhelmingly true.*

Remember when the Lord took the skins from the lambs and wrapped them around the naked bodies of the first couple? That's what He did for Janene and me. "Though your sins are like scarlet, they shall be as white as snow; though they are red like crimson, they shall be as wool" (Isa. 1:18).

Blood-red to snow-white. Only God can do such a thing. I cannot change myself, but oh, the power of God can! When we grant permission to God to change us, one moment we're sinners lost in the muck and mire of sin, condemned to die. But in the next instant we are children of the King, waiting for His coming to take us home!

Janene and I were beginning a new life—but how? Where could we turn? How should we act?

"Christians go to church," Janene reminded me.

So we started attending a friend's church. It was interesting for a while, but soon we realized that the entire service was built on repetition, repetition, repetition. Only rarely did we ever hear anything new.

"Jim and Janene," the church pastor (let's call him Steve) said one day, "My wife and I would like to take you out to dinner."

Dinner with the pastor! I remember thinking. *This is about as close as you can get to God—it's like having dinner with God.*

But soon things turned sour. During dinner we had champagne—actually several bottles of the bubbly. Pastor Steve's wife had been downing her share, and soon some very foul language began to flow from her lips. I took a quick side-glance at Janene. Her expression said the same thing I was thinking—this behavior didn't seem appropriate for people who professed to be leaders of God's church.

At one point during the evening, Steve and I had a few minutes alone.

"Can I ask you a question?" I said.

"By all means."

"What do you think of smoking marijuana?"

I'll never forget his answer.

He shrugged. "All things should be done in moderation."

Moderation? I thought. *Moderation? I can't believe he just said that!* God had just rescued me from a life of drugs which had begun "moderately." Marijuana had tipped me over the edge of a slippery slope, and it was rapidly downhill from there. Don't ever let anyone try to convince you that marijuana doesn't lead to other drugs.

"Janene," I said as we drove home, "maybe it's time we find a new church."
"I agree," she replied firmly. "Let's start looking."

Janene: Our dinner with our "priest" and his wife was truly an awakening. The last few weeks we'd felt we were not sufficiently fed from the church service. Now we were certain this was not where God wanted us to be. We needed to start looking further.

The best part of all of this was that Jim and I were almost always on the same page—maybe not at the exact same moment, but pretty close. God has blessed us with that our entire marriage. Foul language is one thing that really bothers me, and when the pastor's wife started talking like that, neither one of us was happy, especially me. Jim always has honored and respected me, and we both support each other. If one of us has a conviction about something, then the other is in complete support.

Jim: I started reading the Bible again. It was still difficult to understand, but not as much as years ago.

One Sunday afternoon I was sitting at home watching TV, when a commercial about a set of children's books gripped my attention. "Now is your opportunity," said the announcer, "to explore and unfold the many stories of the Bible in words written for children, and in pictures portrayed in beautiful living color."

I was sold. Instantly. *I don't want my son to have to go through all the heartaches I've experienced,* I told myself. *I want him to feel the joy in God that I'm living right now, rather than feeling the full wrath of the deceiver as I'd felt for so many years. Sure, Jason will have to make his own choices, but at least we can provide him some positive guidance.*

"Call right now," the announcer continued. "Pick up your phone and dial this toll-free number to order this beautiful 10-volume set."

And that's just what I did. "Within two weeks," the person on the other end of the line said, "someone will come to your store so you can see the product." I could hardly wait.

True to their word, a fellow came to Jungle Jim's. Amid the shriek of the macaw and the grunts of the animals, he began telling me all about the beauty of the children's Bible set.

"Hey," I said. "I don't have time for the whole story. I just want to buy them."

But he started in again on his spiel.

"OK, OK," I said. "But I'm short on time. Just sign me up."

He just wouldn't listen, but kept talking. Finally I got him quieted down, and he packed his samples back in his case and took my money. As he headed out the door, I thought, *Somebody needs to teach this salesman that when someone's ready to buy, just be quiet, start writing the receipt, and give them what they want!*

But just recently my opinion of this salesman has changed. Janene's comments below—which I read while preparing this chapter—remind me that my mom, who was in the store when the salesman talked with me, was listening to the presentation, and placed an order with him for some other books. So maybe the Lord allowed this man to be long-winded for Mom's benefit.

Janene: When our Bible books arrived, Jim unpacked them and placed them on a little altar we had made. They were beautiful. His mom had also ordered some other books for us. She bought us a large family Bible, and a *Desire of Ages,* and *Bible Readings.** I was so intrigued with *Bible Readings* that I took it to work with me. For two nights a week I served as a relief telephone operator in a small office in Dunsmuir, and once I got my regular work done, I was allowed to read or do anything else I wanted except sleep.

Bible Readings was a great book. I loved it, because it went into so much detail and explained so many things in the Bible. It gave me a lot of information regarding what Scripture tells us about how we should live and what we should eat. This was great, because as a young mother I was very concerned about feeding Jason the right foods. Jim and I also started talking more about the Bible. We continued our church hunt but at that point we couldn't find any denominations that truly followed what Scripture said.

Jim: I couldn't wait for the *Bible Story* set to arrive. When it finally came, I tore open the box and reverently placed the stack of books atop our little family altar. *One day,* I thought, *when Jason is old enough, I'll read these aloud to him.*

Days went by. I decided to open volume 1 and see what was inside, and after reading just one chapter, I was hooked. *This is great stuff!* I thought. *It's written for a 10-year-old, which is just about my age of biblical understanding.* I devoured the chapters one by one, as fast as my baby Christian mind would carry me.

But suddenly I came across some information that seemed really weird.

I read about God providing the repentant Adam and Eve with lamb skins to wear, and how they should teach their offspring that when they sinned they must confess their sins over a lamb and then take its life.

My heart sank.

"Yes, Lord, I am a sinner," I whispered. "Of that I have no doubt. And of course I'll follow Your instructions, even if they seem totally weird."

It was almost Easter. I decided that I had to buy a lamb—soon—confess my sins over it, and slit its innocent throat.

---

*Ellen G. White, *The Desire of Ages* (Nampa, Idaho: Pacific Press Publishing Association, 2005); *Bible Readings for the Home* (Hagerstown, Md.: Review and Herald Publishing Association, 2008).

Chapter 8:

Marvelous Discovery

I was serious.

Where, I asked myself, *am I going to get a lamb? It's not something you can pick up at your local Walmart. I could check the classified ads in the newspaper—but once I found one, then what? The last thing I'm going to do is tell Janene of my plans. She's already thinking that I'm becoming a little "over-the-top" in the religion department. And where could I do this strange act so no one would find out?*

"But I've got to follow You, God!" I prayed desperately. "Help me."

God is so wonderful. He led me step by step during this time of growing. He allowed me to see only so far, to test my resolve and to strengthen me, and then led me to volume 9 of my set of children's *Bible Story* books.* There, in Arthur Maxwell's beautifully clear prose, the plan of salvation was made wonderfully plain to me.

The sweet little lambs in Eden's garden were innocent. They had done nothing worthy of death, but they gave their little lives so that Adam and Eve might live. But they pointed forward to Jesus, who would live a perfect life by the power of the indwelling Holy Spirit—never committing any sin no matter how sorely tempted—but would suffer and die for Adam and Eve's sins, and yours and mine.

It was like a bolt of lightning had struck me. "The innocent Lamb of God—it's Jesus!" I shouted. "*He* suffered and died in my place, on my behalf! He paid the price for my sins! He became my sacrifice and covered my nakedness with His righteousness! Hallelujah!"

This was such an overwhelming revelation that I crumbled at the foot of His cross and wept uncontrollably. In that moment I realized that my sins had killed the spotless Lamb of God. I wielded the hammer that drove the nails deep into His tender, sinless flesh, pinning Him to the wooden cross.

And it wasn't the nails that held Him there, but His love for us. He could have come down anytime He decided to—after all, He was God. But it was

His chosen mission to hang there, naked, bleeding, and dying, so He could save everyone who ever lived. But we too have a choice to make. We must choose to accept Him as the Lord and Savior of our lives, or His sacrifice will mean nothing to us and we will be eternally lost.

Right then and there, that children's book still open before me, I confessed my utter helplessness and hopelessness over the Lamb and earnestly sought His forgiveness. And I knew that His forgiveness was quick, because by His sacrifice He had paid the ultimate ransom for me and you. I now clung to Him as my Savior, Lord, and best Friend. That day, it seemed as though the birds were singing just for me.

And somewhere, a little white northern California lamb, who now would never need to see my face, lived out its days in peace.

And that was only half the story. You see, God doesn't just want us clean on the outside. He wants to remove sin from our lives completely, on the inside as well. And He has the power to make it happen. That's why He told Adam and Eve that He would place enmity between them and the devil's seed (or followers). If they would cooperate, He would come and live within them through the Holy Spirit, and offer them a deep-seated repugnance toward sin, which is what enmity means.

Some people say, "It's not possible to overcome the devil in our lifetime. We'll have to wait until we get to heaven in order to stop falling into every sin-trap the devil lays for us."

To them I say, "Which cosmic being is stronger, God or the devil?" Jesus once said, "With men, it is impossible, but not with God; for with God all things are possible" (Mark 10:27). When we choose to allow the Holy Spirit to live in our body temple—heart and mind—we have invited His authority and dynamite power to defeat the evil that has taken up residence in us. And if we give Him permission, He will go through every room in our "temple"—living room, bedroom, dining room, even the basement!

Let's do a quick fast-forward two years from the moment I knelt with *The Bible Story,* volume 9, in my hands. Now I'm attending a training session which will teach me to become a literature evangelist, a seller of the very books that had changed my life.

"Let's talk about advertising strategies," one of the training team says. "A couple of years ago we created a TV commercial which we aired across part of California. The add offered a toll-free number so people could call and order the 10-volume *Bible Story* set."

My ears perk up.

"However," the trainer continues, "it was a dismal failure. The ad generated only one phone call and one sale."

My mind begins to race. *One call . . . just one call.* It suddenly hits me. *That one call was me! I was the one! God created a TV ad just for me!*

That moment has become a way-marker in my life, a guidepost that shows God's tender care and steady, unfailing love for me. It provides me courage and strength through the rougher, tougher times.

Shortly after the lamb-sacrifice crisis, I began to increase my prayer and study time. I was now praying at least an hour or two every day, and my study time stretched into the night and often early morning.

And I began to ignore Janene.

"I wish," she said with annoyance in her voice, "that I could get between the pages of that book you're reading."

Janene: As Jim began studying the Bible he was like a sponge that couldn't absorb water fast enough. I worked nights and evenings so that our son would be with one of us at all times. Some days when I was working, Jason stayed with my mom. Jim always had his nose in a book—or his body at a prayer meeting. He was talking Bible to anyone and everyone. At times I wondered if our business would survive. Then I began to wonder if our marriage would survive. However, we had made a vow never to divorce. So I did my best to try to keep up with his newfound knowledge.

Jim: She's right. I should have been more sensitive to her. One of the first areas the devil focuses his attacks is on communication between man and woman. That's because he knows that a happy home is formed with a triangle of love—God, husband, and wife, with all three in constant communication.

In quest of a truly Bible-based church I continued denomination-hopping. One evening I was at prayer meeting at a local church. Midway through the discussion I was startled.

"What did you say?" I asked. "Wicked people are going to burn forever in hell?"

Several heads nodded.

"Please help me out here," I pleaded. "Which text are you referring to?"

The discussion continued, but nobody quoted any texts.

"Look, I've got to have Bible proof," I told them.

Again, more talk, but no Bible answers.

"God is love, right?" I asked. "So how could a God of love burn a 70-year-old sinner for billions and billions of years? I mean, our earthly justice system has greater fairness than that!"

Nobody said anything.

"From the texts I've studied," I continued, "it seems that the *effects* of hell-fire will last forever, but sin and sinners will ultimately be destroyed."

The pastor cleared his throat and glanced at the pianist. "Let's sing our closing song," he said. So we did, and then we were dismissed. I had broken up the prayer meeting.

Next day I went to the pastor's home, and quizzed him on every Bible text that talked about God's final judgment on the wicked.

"Where," I asked him, "can I find proof-positive that the wicked will burn forever?"

Again, the pastor ignored his Bible. "Jim," he said, "God gave me a dream. I dreamed I was in heaven standing with all of the redeemed. And across a large gulf stood all the lost in the flames of hell, being tormented for eternity."

"But how could this be?" I asked. "How could that be justice? How could the guy who stole his neighbor's car get the same punishment as the guy who killed dozens of people? How could a God of love be so completely unjust? Where's your Bible proof?"

He looked at a corner of the ceiling for a moment, then turned to face me. "Jim," he said, "I think you should find another church."

Whoa, I thought. *I've been kicked out of a church! This doesn't seem like my idea of the Christian walk. Lord, I am laying my life fully open to You, and I trust Your leading—but where are You leading me?*

Meanwhile, back at my personal Jungle, things were going well. As before, I worked at the store all day, but now I had a new purpose, new drive, and new excitement—to fully understand God's Word and apply it to my life.

I began to see every customer who came through the door as a potential candidate for the kingdom of heaven, and I felt it was my duty to give them the opportunity. Ironically, I had become one of the very people I used to criticize and ridicule. This is typical of people changed by God's grace: "The things I once loved, I now hate; and the things I once hated, I now love" (see *Review & Herald*, April 9, 1889, par. 8).

Janene and I began to talk about religion more often, but I was so on fire that I must have behaved like a huge river of excitement rolling over everything in its path. God was my only topic of interest. I was no longer the man she had married.

We both were getting really discouraged because our search for a church kept running into a brick wall. What we read in the Bible didn't match with what we were hearing from Christians around us.

"Mr. Ayer," a priest told me, "If I were you, I wouldn't bother trying to understand the book of Revelation."

"Why not?"

"John was a mystic," he replied. "He had his head in the clouds. We simply cannot understand that book."

This doesn't make any sense, I remember thinking. *The very name of the book means "to reveal." Why would God allow a book to be named The Revelation if nobody could understand what it was saying?*

"What do we do, Lord?" I prayed. "Have we been wrong in our studies?"

God answered this prayer with His characteristic sense of humor—by bringing me face to face with my greatest earthly fear.

I got a toothache.

---

*Arthur S. Maxwell, *The Bible Story,* vols. 1-10 (Hagerstown, Md: Review and Herald Publishing Association, 1994).

CHAPTER 9:

TRUTH IN THE DENTIST'S CHAIR

"The mighty Jungle Jim is afraid of the dentist's chair?" I can hear my readers say, and I detect a veiled snicker in their tone. "The man who can wrestle a 12-foot anaconda? The man who casually speaks of dealing in African lions? The man who—carefully armed with a garbage can lid and a broom—can even stare the cat Benji in the face and make him wilt?"

Alas, it is true. I dread dental appointments. But the tooth was aching horribly.

OK, I guess I'll have to bite the bullet, I said, though the thought of biting anything made me wince. *Whom shall I call in this emergency?*

Suddenly I remembered that there was a dentist in town who had the reputation of being a "religious nut." So in my hour of crisis I decided to trust my life to someone who hopefully had a close connection with God.

"Yes, Mr. Ayer," said the kindly receptionist when I phoned. "We can see you today."

I hate dentists' offices. I hate the deadly whizzing noises and the crunch of the drill against my teeth. I hate the smell which reached even into the religious dentist's waiting room, where I crouched morosely.

A male voice broke into my misery. "Come in, Mr. Ayer," the dentist said, holding open the door into his lair.

I kept up a nervous small-talk chatter as long as I could, but the moment came when his long needle neared my precious gum line. In desperation, I fired off one more question to try and forestall the stab.

"Doctor," I said as he inserted a latex-gloved finger into my cheek. "Everyone in town thinks you're a religious fanatic."

"Oh?" he said in that absent-minded voice which dentists use when they are starting to forget about you and are focusing on your tooth.

"What do you believe?"

He smiled gently. *Jab!*

"Oughhh!"

Filling my mouth with cotton, he got to work. He had me right where he wanted me. He drilled, then he talked, and then he drilled again. He even asked questions, but as with most dentists he didn't seem to expect answers from someone whose mouth was full of cotton and dentist-finger and drill.

But for the very first time in my adult life, dentists and the pain they caused were not a big deal. I was too fascinated. He was quoting Bible texts and sharing his faith at least as fast as he was drilling. My mind raced along with his. *These are the exact same topics Janene and I have been studying and wondering about,* I remember thinking. An hour later, after a final couple of jaw-vibrating buzzes with the drill, this man had answered every question on our minds. And he did it all from the Bible—and from memory!

And then, as he removed the cotton from my mouth, he launched into a topic that caused me to sit up and take notice. He talked about Sabbath worship. Janene and I had just been arguing about this.

"Saturday," Janene had insisted, "is the day God wants us to worship Him."

I'd shaken my head. "Centuries of Christians can't be wrong. Sunday is the Bible's day of worship."

"All you need to do," she retorted, "is go look at the calendar and see which one is the seventh day of the week, the day God mentions in the Ten Commandments."

Well, she had me there. Sunday was the first day, and Saturday was the seventh day. But now, hearing this dentist talk about this obscure topic, I found myself fascinated.

"Doctor, what church do you go to?"

"Seventh-day Adventist."

Oh, no, I thought. *I've heard of those crazies before. I want nothing to do with them. I've already been mixed up in so many weird things in my life that I sure don't want to start with a new batch.*

I'm not sure whether dentists develop a sixth sense by spending their days communicating with patients who can't talk, but he must have sensed my reaction.

"Worshipping on Saturday isn't in step with what most Christians do," he admitted. "But our top priority is to seek God and follow His revealed will for us as He's set it forth in the Bible. That's our first duty."

He hoisted my chair-back to its upright position. "Why don't you stop by sometime and worship with us?"

"Hmmm," I said. "I'll consider that."

I headed back to the store, feeling less pain than before. I couldn't wait to tell Janene everything that had happened.

"I'll tell you what," she said once I'd finished giving my report. "I'll watch the store this Saturday, and you go to that church and check it out."

"OK," I said. "And I'm going to take my Bible and my notebook with me." You see, I was starting to get a little cocky in my scriptural knowledge. *I've proven every other preacher wrong,* I thought. *I'm gonna get this Adventist preacher, too.*

The Adventists met in a run-down country church with beautiful views of mountains, pastures, and evergreens. I was greeted very graciously, we sang several hymns, had prayer, and then it was time for the sermon. As Providence would have it, the pastor preached on why God expected us to worship on Sabbath.

"The Decalogue's fourth commandment is still in force," he insisted. "In the beginning of earth's history God blessed the seventh day and set it apart for special use by all humanity as a time of special fellowship with Him."

Scribbling hastily, I took a lot of notes. As soon as the service ended, I headed for the library to dig deeper. *Something's wrong somewhere,* I mused. *There had to be some calendar change or something. Maybe a day dropped out and Sunday is really the seventh day.*

I examined every detail of history that had to do with calendar changes. I checked with Mount Palomar Observatory to find if there'd been any celestial changes to affect the day-week cycle. But after extended study I couldn't find anything to cause me to doubt that the seventh day of the week has always been the seventh day of the week.

"Very interesting," I said to Janene when I got home. "Looks like today's sermon was part one of a two-part series on the Sabbath. Guess I'd better go next week too."

"What do you think of what the pastor said?" she asked.

"So far I can't prove him wrong."

Next Saturday I again sat in the pew, flipping to Bible passages and taking notes. In a profound manner, the pastor fitted all the puzzle pieces together and constructed a beautiful picture of God's Sabbath. Adam and Eve kept the Sabbath at the beginning of Creation. Jesus kept it as our example in all things. His disciples observed it, and Isaiah tells us that in heaven all of us will worship God on the Sabbath. "'And it shall come to pass that from one New Moon to another, and from one Sabbath to another, all flesh shall come to worship before Me,' says the Lord" (Isaiah 66:23).

If God is the same yesterday, today, and forever, I thought, remembering Hebrews 13:8, *then why would He do an arbitrary day-switch right in the middle of history? Sabbath in Eden, Sabbath for Jesus, Sabbath for the disciples. Then Sunday for Christians. Then back to Sabbath for all eternity? That seems really strange.*

Second Chance

Let's say you're back in college. You meet a beautiful girl and you invite her out.

"Let's meet at the Golden Jade Chinese Restaurant Saturday afternoon," you suggest. All week long you're thinking about this date and looking forward to it. And when the special day arrives, you go to the restaurant early just to be sure you don't miss her.

Time passes. You keep glancing at your watch. *She's stood me up,* you think. *She's a no-show.*

A couple of days later you spot her on campus. "Hey," you say, trying to keep the disappointment out of your voice. "I waited more than an hour for you on Saturday. What happened?"

She smiles cheerfully. "Oh, I thought I'd meet you on Sunday instead. I didn't think it mattered that much. One day is as good as the next."

How would you feel?

Actually, the real question is, How does *God* feel? You see, He gave us the Sabbath not only as a special memorial of Creation but as a perpetual "date" between Him and His people. And for many centuries, most Christians have been no-shows. And because of that, many are missing out on incredible blessings from their best Friend.

"Those Adventists are right, Janene," I said soberly when I returned from church. "I cannot prove them wrong. You know what that means, right?"

"The store," she said, reading my mind. "Saturday is the week's biggest income-producing day."

Chapter 10:

Money, or Relationship?

I nodded. "If we close on Saturday, that could mean financial ruin. Everything you and I have worked for could be lost."

My mom and dad, who happened to be with us right then, were alarmed. "If you close Saturdays, you won't survive! Why would you want to do that?"

"But if it's the Sabbath . . . " Janene began.

"No 'if's' about it," I said. "Saturday *is* the Sabbath. You figured that out before I did, remember?" I thought for a moment, my mind paging through a mental calendar. "I've got it." I went to the telephone and dialed the local radio station.

"Begin advertising that, starting in eight weeks, Jungle Jim's will be closed on Saturdays," I told the ad person.

"Eight weeks?" Janene asked when I hung up the phone.

"Right," I said. "Let's keep it open Saturdays until we're through the Fourth of July. It's a huge tourist time. That'll give us a big boost financially, and we can give some of that money to the Lord."

The next morning I woke up feeling terrible. *What am I doing, bargaining with God?* I asked myself. *What's more important—money, or my relationship with the Lord?*

I grabbed for the phone and dialed the radio ad man again. "Change that commercial," I ordered him. "Starting *this week,* Jungle Jim's will be closed on Saturdays and open on Sundays." And even though I could already feel my stomach tightening against a financial slump, I felt 100 percent better. Janene and I had chosen to serve our Lord and deny the voice of the devil, regardless of the consequences.

And how did it turn out?

If you've had any experience at all following the Lord, you know already. Sunday became our best day of the week—and far exceeded any income that Saturdays had ever produced. What a witness that was to my mom and dad!

And did we keep going to the Adventist church? Of course we did—and we're *still* going to the Seventh-day Adventist church because we *must* go. And if Janene and I ever were to find another denomination who's teaching more sound biblical truth than our church, we'd be obligated to go there.

That's because attending church isn't about going because your friends are there, or because you like the music, or because the pastor is handsome and dynamic. *Attending church is about following truth wherever it leads.* Jesus said, "You shall know the truth, and the truth shall make you free" (John 8:32). I choose to be free—therefore I must go where truth is presented. That's why I am compelled to be a Seventh-day Adventist—the seventh day is the biblical Sabbath, and I believe with all my heart in the soon "advent" of Jesus my Lord and Savior.

If you're a veteran Adventist you're going to give a horrified hiccup at how Janene and I celebrated Sabbaths at the start. We hadn't officially joined the church yet—but we attended faithfully. And we still had a lot to learn about how God wanted us to keep His day holy. So after the worship service was over we'd generally go the supermarket and buy wine or champagne and some cheese. Then we'd spend the day at the park, relaxing. Isn't God so kind and gentle in His care and leading? He takes us one step at time.

But one day—just after we'd stocked up with our favorite champagne—the Lord led us to the verses which told us that our bodies were meant to be the home of the Holy Spirit, and that alcohol numbed the delicate senses of the brain, and hindered our ability to hear and act upon the Spirit's voice. So out went the champagne and everything else alcoholic.

I still get a chuckle out of our first rather jerky attempt to help our little church. The building, as I mentioned, was run-down. Paint had peeled away from the ceiling and walls, and the vinyl floor was tattered and torn.

"This isn't what the house of God should look like," Janene and I told each other. "Why should our own home look better than God's?" We weren't members yet, but we decided to do something about it.

As a surprise.

Did I hear a horrified gasp at the word "surprise"?

Remember wood paneling? You do if you're old enough. These glossy quarter-inch-thick by eight-foot by four-foot sheets could be overlaid on almost any surface and make it look like new. So early one Sabbath morning when no one was looking, I paced off the entire sanctuary, then calculated the number of sheets it would take to refinish the entire room.

As it happened, the lumberyard had a huge sale going on, so one Friday we loaded the truck with lots of paneling. Late that evening under cover of darkness we arrived at the deserted church and unloaded everything into a huge stack directly in front of the main church doors. That's right—the paneling pile squarely blocked the entrance.

On top of the stack we placed a hammer and a box or two of nails. And then we committed a major sin (at least that's what one dear saint thought). Under the hammer I placed a letter I had typed. It read:

"My dear children: I have grown this wood in My forest. I have placed it here for you to use in order to beautify My sanctuary. Thank you."

And I signed it, "Your loving Savior Jesus."

As luck would have it, the person who found the letter the next morning was a gray-haired old saint I'll call Bessie. "That is absolute *blasphemy*!" she gasped. (The only reason you're reading this is that Bessie has passed to her rest in the Lord. Perhaps in heaven I can finally reveal to her that I was the blasphemer.)

That Sabbath morning we made sure we were the last ones to show up. When we got there, all the wood had been neatly restacked inside in the hallway. But no one said a word about it all morning. And the next Sabbath everybody was silent about it too. Finally I couldn't stand it.

"What's all that paneling doing there?" I asked casually.

"We don't know," someone said. "It just showed up here one morning with a note attached."

"A note?" I repeated.

"Someone typed a note and signed Jesus' name to it. Boy, it sure got Bessie upset!"

I paused for a moment. Then, as though the idea had suddenly just occurred to me, I said, "Well, shouldn't we put it up?"

"Hey, that's an idea," someone said. "Why don't you head up the task?"

Suddenly, even though I wasn't a member, I was the chair of the brand-new building committee. And I could sense the Spirit of the Lord right there with us as we swung into our renovation project.

During construction, a man moved to the area and started attending.

"I like what's happening here," he said. "The Lord just laid a burden on my heart to donate new carpeting for you." A little later, somebody in town offered deep discounts on new lighting. Then a member worked with a local supplier to purchase custom drapes for our huge windows at an equally huge saving.

"I don't think people like Bessie can hear the sermon very well," I said one day. "I'm going to look into a sound system." So I headed down to a local electronics store. But when the store's employee told me what a system would cost, I hung my head.

"Sorry," I said. "My church isn't going to be able to swing it."

I walked toward the door, but as my hand reached out to push it open, a voice called out, "Wait!"

I turned, and a man who'd been standing near the counter beckoned me over.

"I overheard what you were talking about," he said with a smile. "God placed a burden upon my heart several days back. It was revealed to me that someone would enter my life with a need of some kind. And when I heard your story, I knew God placed me here this morning to give you a sound system." It turned out that he was the store's equipment dealer for sound systems!

By the way, don't shy away from the idea of God speaking to us today. He did it throughout the Old and New Testaments, and He does it in modern times. And the way to cultivate this communication is to have a regular time of Bible study and prayer. This is where heaven and earth meet. This is where prayer and study become a deep personal exchange between Creator and created, an ebb and flow of thoughts, of ideas, of sharing as friend to friend.

One by one Janene and I were learning the exciting, heart-satisfying principles which most Adventists take for granted. We learned to tithe—to return 10 percent of our increase to the Lord. Malachi 3:8 told us that withholding tithe is robbing God. Verses 8 to 11 also talk about freewill offerings. What it boiled down to was, *Could we really trust God with money that up to then we'd thought was ours?*

Recognize these people? Focus on their last names if you need a clue: J. C. Penney, William Colgate, Henry Heinz, Milton Hershey, and many others. All were tithepayers. They took God up on His challenge—and they discovered that when God says it, you can believe it. Janene and I have found that God keeps His promise and pours out abundant blessings—blessings that are custom-made for you. Maybe they will come in the form of money, maybe in better health, maybe in personal peace. God never runs out of ways to bless us as we follow His bidding, and He tailors each one to what would really and most deeply make us happy.

"When are you going to be baptized?" church members started asking me.

"When Janene is ready," I always answered.

I wanted to wait for her. But I wasn't really waiting. The word "waiting" indicates that someone is standing passively by. Not me. I loved every minute of our new life, and I was trying to drag Janene right along with me. OK, let's get real. I was hounding her and pestering her to death. I was so on fire that I just had to share with her every new thought, every new scripture, every tiny detail—whether or not she wanted to hear it!

I was overjoyed the day she agreed to go with me to the pastor's home for Bible studies.

Only to have her feel as though she'd been punched in the stomach.

Janene: Even though Jim studied a lot while I was at work in the evenings, the pastor wanted to have Bible studies with both of us before we were baptized. So we set a date to travel to his home in Yreka which was about 40 miles from our home. He and his wife were very gracious upon our arrival, and we sat and visited for a few minutes prior to the study. Then we had prayer and the study began.

The first thing he told me—even before we had opened our Bibles—was, "Young lady, you're going to take off your wedding ring, stop working on Sabbath, and stop wearing those short skirts."

Well, needless to say, this went over like a lead balloon. I burst into tears, and immediately got up and walked out of that living room and sat in the car. And I never returned to that home, ever again.

If I can offer one word of advice to anyone giving a Bible study to anyone: this is *not* how you begin a study. I did not want any part of this church, and especially this pastor. Jim soon came out to the car, and I don't remember much else of that day.

Chapter 11:

Baptism and Catfishing

"Jim and Janene," Roland, one of our church elders asked one day. "Would you like to come to camp meeting with us?"

"What's camp meeting?" I asked.

"Hundreds of people come from all over, and we camp out in the redwoods," he said. "We listen to great preachers all week, sing a lot, and have a great time."

Janene's soul-wounds had healed a bit by this time, and "camping" and "redwoods" and "great time" sounded good to us.

"Sure," we said.

That Friday we headed off with our new friends through wonderful summer weather and great scenery. The sun had just dipped below the hills when we passed through a quaint little town.

"Too bad it's already Sabbath," Roland said mildly to his wife. "We could have stopped and grabbed a cold soda."

In the back seat, Janene looked at me and I looked at her. She whispered, "We're not supposed to *buy* things on Sabbath?" "I guess not," I whispered back. Now *that's* the way "testing truth" should be shared—*gently,* with the Holy Spirit providing a natural way.

It was dark when we arrived, but we managed to get our tents up and then snuggled in for the night. Our sleeping bags provided the perfect barrier against the cool night air, while our noses sniffed the pungent scents of the redwood forest.

Morning was like nothing else I'd ever experienced. Gentle slivers of sunlight broke through the mighty evergreen giants. Stepping outside the tent, I suddenly found myself standing in God's cathedral of nature. Soft, persuasive organ music sounded from somewhere, lifting my heart to heaven. The music, the trees, the experience . . . it was magical . . . no, it was heavenly!

Roland Hegstad was the speaker for the main meeting, and I can still see him behind the outdoor pulpit, surrounded by a mighty stand of redwoods. He preached powerfully, and as he neared the climax God spoke through him to deliver one of the most eloquent invitations to accept Christ that I have ever heard.

"If you want to respond to this love," he concluded, "if you want to surrender all to the Lord, stand up. Right now."

In an instant, Janene was on her feet.

Praise God! I rejoiced, as I jumped up to stand beside her. *God, and God alone, has melted her heart, and now the two of us are ready as husband and wife to unite with God's people.*

Did we know everything? No. Did we understand all there was to understand about God and Bible? No. But we studied and prepared for baptism. We surrendered all that the Spirit had asked us to replace with better things, better ways. And finally the wonderful day of our baptism arrived.

"Shall we gather at the river," our church friends sang that November Sabbath. And we were indeed standing on the banks of a river—but few of these dear people knew the truth. We were being baptized beside the very river, and at the exact spot, where Janene and I had sat on the bank dangling our feet in the water, smoking marijuana, and vowing to love each other forever when I proposed to her! Can you imagine what this says to us about our delightful, loving, good-humored heavenly Father? We know that He and His angels were celebrating with us on that crisp November day.

We were now full-fledged members of the Seventh-day Adventist Church. Janene and I started looking for people to study the Bible with, and soon had a perpetual stream of Bible studies going.

And that's how we met Don and April.

One afternoon a tall, good-looking young couple about our age strolled in to Jungle Jim's. "We need some myna bird food," one of them said, so I talked them through the products and left them alone to decide.

A Buddhist monk also happened to be in the store at the same time, and as soon as he left, the young couple approached us. The man asked, "Who was that person dressed in the strange outfit?"

I shared some information about Buddhism with them and listened carefully to their response. (I've learned that listening, rather than just lecturing, is an important part of understanding where God is at work, so that we can join Him in that work in an empathetic way.)

God's working on this couple, I decided as I talked with them. *And the two of them and I are really hitting it off together. Time to join God at work.*

"I'm Jim," I said, offering my hand. "But you probably knew that."

"I'm Don," the man said, "and this is April."

"Hey," I said, "how would you folks like to go catfishing some night?"

Their eyes widened, and they looked at each other. "Sure."

The neat thing about catfishing is that it involves hours and hours of waiting (and talking), and then a few minutes of fish-catching. Don and April joined Janene and me at many a late-night catfishing adventure, and the four of us really hit it off. (And though Janene and I were baby Adventists, we knew that catfish weren't "clean"—so any we caught we gave to Don and April. Well, I didn't say we were perfect!)

I like to call this "fireside evangelism." If you want to win people to the Lord, spend time with them. Invite them to join you by the fire, and just relax. Get to know them, take time to become involved in their lives, become friends—and then, when you gently share God's love, they will be receptive. It's been years since I actually took anybody catfishing (!), but Janene and I still do fireside evangelism.

"Janene," I chuckled, "we're spending so much time with Don and April that I don't know whether we're converting them or they're converting us."

After two years of friendship-building, we invited them to an evangelistic series.

"OK," they said. But I got the impression that they weren't overly excited. And sure enough, they showed up—a bit late, but they made it. *Lord,* Janene and I prayed, *please bring them back for night two.* Back they came, and for night three as well.

Four days into the meeting they came to our house. Both had bad colds and they gave them to us!

"Hey, guys," I said in mock annoyance. "If you were really good friends with us, you'd keep that garbage to yourself."

"What garbage?" Don asked.

"Those colds of yours."

"Well," April piped up, "it's a small price to pay for two souls, isn't it?"

I did a double-take, and stared at her. "What did you say?"

She giggled. "Isn't it a small price to pay for two souls?"

Now Janene and I were both staring.

"Seriously," April said. "Don and I gave our hearts to the Lord tonight."

Talk about excited! This was a bolt out of the blue. We had worked with the Barnts for so long, prayed so much, studied so hard—and now it was time for celebration.

"Let me tell you the rest of the story," April continued.

Janene and I had been right when we suspected that Don and April weren't all that interested in coming to that first meeting, but had only said yes to be polite. Opening night found them in their truck heading north toward another engagement in a distant city. But as they drove, they found themselves talking about the friendship and love Janene and I had shown to them.

As they talked, April suddenly glanced at her watch. "Don."

"What?"

"What shall we do?"

Don knew what she was thinking, and sighed. "Jim and Janene are really looking forward to seeing us at that meeting," he said. "I don't want to let them down."

"Neither do I. But I don't want to give up our own plans for tonight either."

They drove on in silence for a couple of minutes. But love and friendship finally won out.

"Don," April said, "let's turn the truck around."

Don found a wide spot in the road, turned that pickup around, and headed toward their destiny—which would lead them to the pastoral ministry and then full-time evangelism. Through their efforts, thousands of lives would be changed for eternity.

Janene: The night Don and April told us they'd given their hearts to God was one of the highest moments in Jim's and my Christian experience. We'd known drug highs, but never the high that we felt that night. Two people who had become very special to us had made a life-changing decision, and after they left us that evening we could not contain our excitement. We were jumping up and down, tears running down our faces, smiling from ear to ear. It was an experience like no other—and once you've gone through it, you hunger to share our most precious Lord with everyone else. And we didn't realize at the time that this couple would remain close friends with us for the rest of our lives.

Jim: Before I continue, I've got to share another amazing story.

Don and April would eventually attend Union College in Lincoln, Nebraska, where April would study art and Don would take theology. On fire for Jesus, he shared his joy and love for his Savior with everyone he came in contact with there at the school.

One person he shared his story with was a young assistant professor of English, who had grown up in the Adventist church. "I had always known about Jesus," the professor says. "I knew that He died for me on the cross, and I loved Him for that. But when I met Don and April, I was deeply impressed at how comfortable and familiar they were with the Savior. It was like I had seen Jesus at a distance, but they had welcomed Him into every part of their life, and talked naturally about Him as though He were a personal friend.

"I'd never met, up close, anybody like Don and April before," he continues. "For the first time I sensed the joy of someone who wasn't raised Christian, but who came to know that Jesus is not only real, but wants to be incredibly close and companionable. This caused me to reevaluate my own relationship with the Savior. It was life-changing for me."

This young man was not only an English teacher but also a budding author. One of his first published books would be called *Pilgrimage.* It was Don and April's story.

Recently the Review and Herald Publishing Association asked me to share our own story. After almost 200 pages I discovered that writing about my personal life was harder than any other writing I'd ever done. So I gave it to Jeannette Johnson, the book acquisitions editor, and said, "I know there's a story in here, but it needs real help. If you want to get someone to tighten it up and make it better, feel free."

Jeannette said she knew someone who could help, and that he lived in the Seattle area. As it turned out, I would be speaking at an Adventist camp meeting there in two weeks, and I could meet with him. Jeannette sent the manuscript to him by e-mail.

The author's name was Maylan Schurch, so I called him and began to discuss the book.

"Do you know what?" he said. "As I started reading through your manuscript, things started sounding familiar. Then when I got to the 'Jungle Jim' part, I knew that you were the same person who had had such an effect on Don and April. I was the one who wrote *Pilgrimage*!"

Isn't the leading of God wonderful? This English professor-turned-pastor who could trace his own deepening relationship with Christ through Don and April and, through them, back to Janene and me, is now helping us tell our own story!

Not long after our own baptism, Tom, a member of the church board, came to me. "Jim," he said, "we would like for you to be a deacon."

"Wow," I said. "I'd love to."

"On one condition," he said soberly.

"What's that?"

"That you stop handing out Baptist literature!"

Dad's life was spared during the Battle of the Bulge when a Luftwaffe plane dropped a bomb on a church where he and other soldiers were hiding.

My dad, James Ayer, Sr., on furlough from service with the 101st Airborne Division during World War II, stands with his young wife, Jeanette (she was 16 when they married) in front of their California home.

All dressed up for church. Mom decided I needed some religion, so she sent me to the local Baptist church until I became old enough to refuse to go.

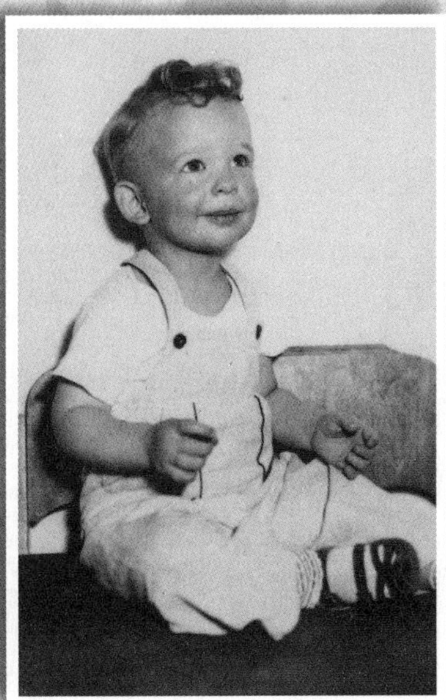

Here I am at 18 months, ready for a life of excitement!

My first car: a red Olds Cutlass. I bought it—then the season's first major snowstorm kept me from driving my "muscle car" for two agonizing weeks!

Beverly Janene Thompson, the stunning blond the Lord brought into my life, serves punch at a reception.

I was my high school's student business manager, surrounded by the all-girl yearbook team. Tough job, but somebody had to do it.

I represented the freshman class in my college's student government association (kneeling, second from left). Sandi, who would become the mother of my son Dan, stands behind my right shoulder. In the group of three seated girls, the two on either end are the twins who led a Christian youth group and tried to interest me in spiritual things.

On a weekend campout. (I'm in my mid-30s.)

At the end of a stressful day of politics and real estate there was always our hot tub—and a breathtaking view of Mount Shasta just beyond my feet.

Here I am during my "hippie druggie" period, posed against some magnificent canyon scenery, my left hand cradling a belt pouch that holds a 9-millimeter Smith & Wesson pistol.

Janene and I (left) and our good friends April and Don Barnt, whom we first met when they came to Jungle Jim's for myna bird food. Two years later the Barnts were baptized, and the four of us formed a witnessing team to encourage parents of kids who used drugs.

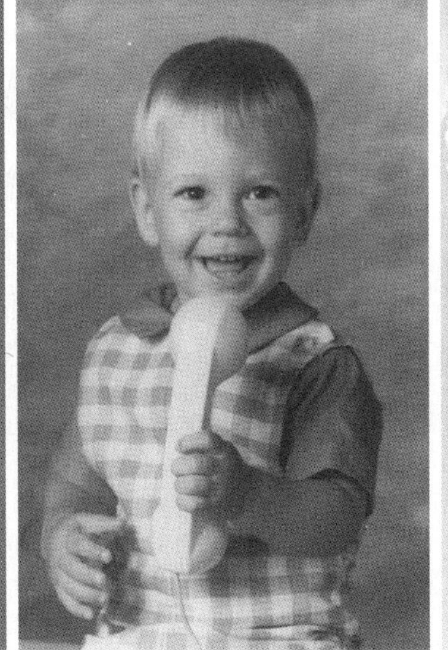

My beautiful (and long-lost) first son, Dan, age 2, posing for the camera with "his" phone in hand.

On the sidewalk just outside Jungle Jim's Pet Shop with a Malayan Sun bear cub.

Right to left: Janene, daughter Meriah, son Jason, and I having a great time in Cozumel, Mexico.

Here's
Dan holding a pyrotechnics bomb! Dan was assisting with a Seattle fireworks display.

Notice the two smiles. (Meriah's is delighted; Jason's is a bit more forced.) Who needs all these dollies, anyhow?

I am discussing various issues with presidential candidate Pat Buchanan. As president of what was voted the most active grassroots organization in the western U.S., I was thrust into fairly heady company.

Janene (right)
is astride her beloved horse, Windswept Carla, and Meriah rides Carla's daughter, Fancee Farrah. Carla's son Shilo, who has offspring all over the world, died in the spring of 2009 at age 26. Carla lived to be 38.

Janene and I attended a congressional luncheon in Washington, D.C., with our friend Pam Herger, at which Dan Rather spoke. Afterward we posed with Dan and Pam, whose husband, Wally, is a United States congressman.

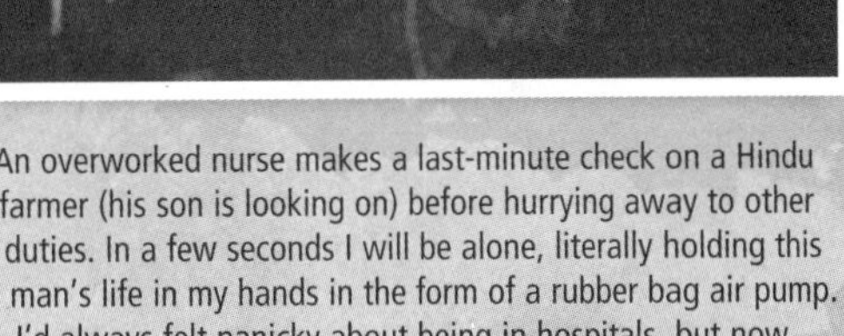

An overworked nurse makes a last-minute check on a Hindu farmer (his son is looking on) before hurrying away to other duties. In a few seconds I will be alone, literally holding this man's life in my hands in the form of a rubber bag air pump. I'd always felt panicky about being in hospitals, but now the Lord gave me peace.

Her family's finances had kept Janene from becoming a nurse, a teacher, or a dental assistant. On our mission trips she's fulfilled all three roles—and that of pharmacist, as well. Her smile says it all.

I've always been terrified of dentists' offices, but after taking so many medical and dental teams on mission trips, I've learned how to clean teeth—and even to extract them—and have become something of a practicing developing-nations dentist!

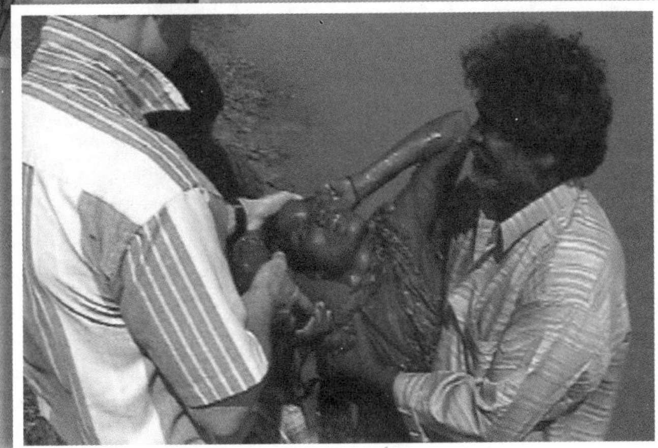

At the end of an evangelistic series that I preached in Cuddapah, India, a young baptismal candidate was suddenly possessed by a demon. He tried to drown her by holding her under the water, but divine intervention brought her to the surface, where I commanded the demons to depart in the name of Jesus. Calm came over her, and she walked up the riverbank on her own.

Janene stands with her oxcart driver on one of our India mission trips.

Janene and Bithica share a hug in front of a Maranatha school and orphanage in Bangladesh. We discovered just in time that this 10-year-old girl's parents were planning to sell her into slavery (or even prostitution) to get enough money to provide for their other children. We paid her price ($10), put her in school, and assisted her family.

Adventist World Radio president Ben Schoun poses with a group of devoted AWR listeners in northeast India. The trays in the foreground contain silkworms similar to the Sabbathkeeping worms whose story I tell in the book.

This woman's husband and two of her sons were sent to jail for murdering the third son. In prison one of the sons began listening to Adventist World Radio and shared the gospel message with the wives they had left behind. This woman, once a strong Hindu, has now made her home a Christian spiritual center where people come from miles around to find physical and spiritual healing.

As I was returning from preaching a major evangelistic series in the Dominican Republic, the Lord arranged that Amazing Facts speaker/director Doug Batchelor would be on the same flight. This led to my becoming A-Facts' vice president for public affairs and global events, responsible for organizing several worldwide satellite events, including "The Most Amazing Prophecies," hosted by Andrews University.

Gary Gibbs, Doug Batchelor, and I pause in front of the Notre Dame Cathedral on our way to Africa for evangelistic meetings.

On one of my *Making Waves* TV programs, I interview a double murderer from Burma who was won to Christ through Adventist World Radio.

You just never know whom you'll meet strolling the streets of Moscow. I've come upon no less than Joseph Stalin and one of the czars!

Well, it's slower than an Olds Cutlass, but a whole lot more exotic!

A cheerful "holy man" of India, whom we encountered while filming a *Making Waves* broadcast.

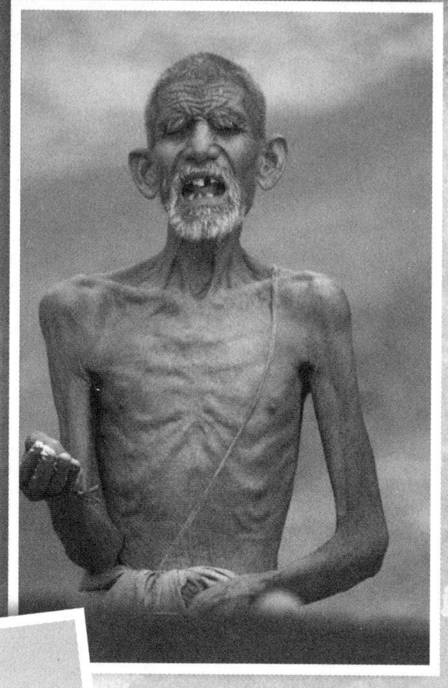

And, by contrast, a near-skeletal beggar. It's not unusual to see sorrow like this on a regular basis in India.

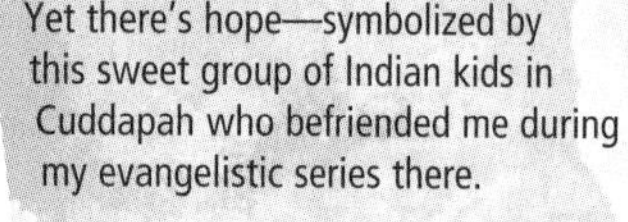

Yet there's hope—symbolized by this sweet group of Indian kids in Cuddapah who befriended me during my evangelistic series there.

Here's
an absolutely blissed-out
Grandpa Jim with Jason's daughter, Alexis (left), and Meriah's daughter, Madison.

CHAPTER 12:

ON FIRE FOR GOD

I grinned. "OK, Tom," I said, "I'll stop passing out Baptist literature." Then mimicking his own sober tone, I said, "Under one condition."

"What's that?"

"That you provide me with enough Adventist literature to take its place!"

What had happened was that our little church group did not have one single piece of literature to hand out to people who might be interested in the Adventist church. I was so on fire to share my faith that I hunted around and found some powerful little Baptist tracts. True, the doctrine was incorrect in some spots, but the Bible basics were valid and well-presented. I simply corrected the errors with a pen and then passed them out.

Tom grinned. "OK," he said. "We'll make it happen." Soon the treasurer called to say that I could buy all the literature I could use.

I started by purchasing month-old *Signs of the Times* magazines for a dime apiece, a thousand copies at a time. My next challenge was how to get them handed out. Though our little church group numbered only 25 members, God rallied a small but faithful "band of brothers" who went out with me every single Sabbath, door-to-door. By the end of each month we would reach the bottom of our *Signs* stack, and it was time for the following month's shipment. We "farmed" those 1,000 homes for an entire year through rain, sunshine, and deep snow. At the end of the year we gave each family a *Steps to Christ** with a Bible study card included.

Our response rates were off the charts. There was no way we could handle all the studies that came in. Today, when I hear church members say that no one is interested in Bible studies any more, or that evangelism is dead, it makes me sad. Remember, it was God who created God-hunger within humanity—and in every community there are people hungering for a word from the Lord.

I'm going to jump ahead in my story to tell you a personal example of how true this is. Years later I attended a weekend seminar by a Bible instructor.

"I have a wonderful method of helping my students find people to study the Bible with," he told us. "I teach a Bible-marking seminar in my church, and the members learn how to highlight and reference the doctrines in the Bible. When the seminar is done, I promise them a framed graduation certificate—but before they get that certificate they have to go out and actually give a Bible study to someone. And here's where it gets interesting.

"Naturally my students get all worried. 'Where are we going to find Bible studies?' they wonder. I just tell them to go to their hairdresser, mechanic, store clerk, produce person—someone they have regular contact with. 'Would you help me?' I tell them to say. 'I've been taking a special Bible-marking class at my church, and I want to graduate, but I can't until I give someone a Bible study. I could really use your help. Would you mind?'"

The Bible instructor paused and looked around at our group of 40 pastors and lay leaders.

"Tomorrow's the last day of this seminar," he said. "So I am going to challenge you to go out and get a Bible study by tomorrow morning."

There were several uneasy murmurs. "A lot of us don't even live in this area," somebody said. "How are we going to find a Bible study?"

"Let's see your hands," the instructor said calmly. "Who will give a study by tomorrow using this method?"

A few hands went up.

"I'm not letting you off the hook," he continued. "Come on, now. Who *else* will get a Bible study by tomorrow?"

He had to give the call three times before I finally raised my hand. In all, 19 out of the 40 either believed what he was saying—or had been shamed into saying they'd try.

Boy, I've blown it now, I remember thinking as I left the meeting. *Where am I ever going to find a Bible study in a strange city—and find it overnight?*

But on the way to the car, God gave me an idea. My daughter had married Roger, a nice young man who, to his own way of thinking, considered himself a Christian. But when I had begun to talk with him about Bible topics, he politely let me know that he'd had enough, and that I wasn't to talk to him about God any more. So I had honored his request.

Hmmm, I wondered. *Would Roger bite on this idea?* I sent up a little prayer as I sat in my car and dialed my cell phone.

"Roger! Hi," I said, and after a bit of chitchat I continued. "I'm attending a training conference, and—well, I hate to say this, but I think I really put myself out on a limb."

"How do you mean?" Roger asked.

"Well, the presenter challenged us to go out and find someone to study the Bible with by tomorrow. I finally raised my hand, right there in front of my peers. Roger, would you help me? If I don't get a Bible study by tomorrow morning, I'm really going to look stupid."

Roger burst out laughing. "Sure," he said. "I'll help you."

So right there in the car, on the cell phone, five minutes after leaving my seminar, I had my Bible study. And Roger? He's now an elder in the Seventh-day Adventist church—and preaches some good sermons!

Does this method work? *Oh yes.* Are there Bible studies right around the corner from you? *Oh yes.* The next morning at the seminar, we shared our experiences of the previous evening. The 19 people who'd raised their hands had obtained commitments for 20 Bible studies—in less than 24 hours!

Now let's rewind back to our *Signs* magazine handout. Bible studies were happening everywhere. Our 25-member Adventist church had caused our community to sit up and take notice. One day the entire front page of the local newspaper had a photo of our church building with the caption: "This church houses one of the most active congregations in the south county. Can you guess who they are?"

A year earlier Janene and I were able to attend a series of evangelistic meetings presented by Clifton Walter and Bernie Paulsen. We'd become friends with this wonderful team, and I invited them to do a series in our area the following year. They agreed, and it was now time to start our advertising blitz and rent the large military armory to hold the meetings.

How ironic, I mused the night the meetings opened. *Just a few years ago I had rented this very same armory for a very different reason. I'd hired a well-known rock band called Syndicate of Sound to perform a concert. That night, a thousand wild, drinking college students got their ears blown off and their minds ruined. But tonight the crowd is hearing the words of eternal life—and in that crowd sits my grandmother, my mom and dad, Janene's mom, and Don and April.*

At the end of that year of *Signs* distribution, followed by *Steps to Christ* and the Bible studies, 18 people were baptized into the family of God. One of these was my grandmother, who'd been raised in the Dutch Reformed church in Holland. The number of baptisms almost doubled the number of people in our church. God is good!

But trouble laid ahead—trouble in our marriage.

---

*Ellen G. White, *Steps to Christ* (Hagerstown, Md.: Review and Herald Publishing Assoc., 1973).

Chapter 13:

Honey on the Floor

Part of our problem was that Janene and I tended to accept new Bible truth at different speeds.

Take Ellen White, for example. When I heard that the Adventist church believed that Mrs. White had a special gift from God, I had no problem with that. With every book of hers I read, I became more settled in the belief that she was a prophet—because every word she wrote (even the ones which dug into some pet sin of mine) was designed to lift me closer to my Redeemer.

Janene wasn't so sure about the "prophet" claim. Once in a while I would read her a few paragraphs from one of Ellen White's books, but it didn't seem to make much difference.

Janene: I'd been raised in the Christian Science church, and I had heard all about Mary Baker Eddy and how she said that you had to train your mind to take complete control over your body. So when we first joined the church and I came face to face with the writings of another prophet, I was very skeptical. I took all of this "Ellen White stuff" with a grain of salt. *The Bible is my book,* I decided, *and that's what I'm going to follow.*

Jim: Not a day too soon, a man named Rene Noorbergen wrote a book that changed the life of many people. Noorbergen was an experienced correspondent and journalist who had authored a book, *My Life and Prophecies*, with Jeanne Dixon. After much research on the life of Ellen White, he published *Ellen G. White: Prophet of Destiny.*

As of 2000 Ellen White was the most-translated female nonfiction author in the history of literature, as well as the most-translated American nonfiction author of either gender. Even though she had only a third-grade education, she wrote more than 5,000 periodical articles, as well as 40 books including *Steps to Christ, The Desire of Ages,* and *The Great Controversy.*

Rene Noorbergen developed what he called a prophetic accuracy quotient (PAQ) and used it to rate psychics and so-called prophets by how many predictions they made that came true. Some rated as high as 80 percent, which sounds good—except if God gave them the information that meant that God was wrong 20 percent of the time. That's not the God *I* worship! My God knows the future—and can step into and out of time as He wishes.

As Janene paged through the book her curiosity was on the alert. *How well,* she wondered, *did Ellen White score on the PAQ?* It wasn't long before she found the answer—100 percent according to Noorbergen's personal scorecard! By the time she'd finished the book's 235 pages, her heart and mind were changed forever. Ellen White was God's prophet for our day and time in earth's history.

However, just because Janene and I became Christians—and eventually ended up on the same page when it came to our beliefs—this didn't mean that we were protected from troubles and heartaches. These things happen in a world of sin and sorrow. But if we let Him, God can use even these trials and troubles to draw us closer to Him, to soften our rough spots, and get rid of the evil within us.

One day after Janene and I had been married for a while, she said to me in a curt tone, "All the fun has gone out of our marriage." And with that, she headed to the bathroom to take a shower.

No fun? I thought. *You just watch. I'll show you fun.*

I headed for the kitchen, grabbed the honey jar out of the cupboard, and spread a thick layer of honey on the vinyl floor directly in front of the bathroom door. *When Janene comes out of the bathroom, fresh from her shower,* I thought fondly, *she'll get stuck in the honey—and presto! No more stale marriage.*

It's a guy thing.

I waited expectantly for the grand moment. Janene opened the bathroom door and stepped into the honey with her wet feet. She slipped, and her sweetened heels rose nearly as high as her head, and the next thing I knew, she was flat on her back, stuck to the honey.

To this day if you put me under interrogation and asked me what I was hoping would happen, I wouldn't be able to tell you. But that was not it.

There was no immediate reaction from the shell-shocked body lying motionless on the sticky vinyl floor, but it soon spoke. And let us just say that it was a long while before Janene saw the humor in my attempt to bring "fun" back into our marriage.

Janene: Jim and I loved each other (and I loved him even after the honey-on-the-vinyl adventure), but we are both "only" children. Even if one partner is an only child, that's challenging for a marriage, let alone both! Many factors contributed to stress in our relationship, and the devil—who is always ready to do anything he can to take our eyes off Christ—was right there to get between us.

Beware, all you couples out there. Don't let the evil one have that power over your relationship. At the first sign of a problem, sink to your knees and ask for divine intervention to rebuke the devourer of your marriage.

Jim: Even though we were having trouble, we believed that marriage was for better or for worse, and that it should be a lifelong commitment. We had not started our marriage the way our Lord wanted us to—we'd been on drugs and alcohol—but we were now Christians, and we figured God could do something. He does have a way of working out "irreconcilable differences," and it was not His desire that we separate. If the fire was there in the beginning, it must still be smoldering within us, somewhere.

"Let's find a good Seventh-day Adventist counselor," we told each other, and eventually we found a very nice woman counselor five hours away.

Janene: Even before we married, Jim and I had made a commitment not to divorce, so when we started counseling with this woman, I was scared that she might tell us that we needed to separate.

Well, that wasn't the case. She was so wise and understanding, and she knew exactly what we both needed. Our problems were fairly normal ones, with fairly normal answers.

"Jim, you own two cars, right? Well, if Janene is late getting ready for church and you argue over it, each of you drive one of the cars so you can each get to church when you're able to. And yes, Janene *does* need a washer and a dryer and a refrigerator—they *are* necessary items to run a home."

And she took my side on my most important issue.

"Jim," she said, "you should never ask Janene to give up her horse."

My horse, I believe, has helped me stay sane! And since that session with the counselor, Jim has been very patient with me and my steeds, even though he is deathly allergic to them. And he has maintained this attitude even though in later years I owned close to 20 horses at one time.

Our counseling sessions lasted right around six months and we were given several keys to grow our marriage closer and closer. I believe that every couple can benefit from some kind of counseling or marriage enrichment no matter how great they believe their marriage is.

Jim: I really appreciated our counselor. One day she took me aside and had a long talk with me. "Jim," she said, "here's the situation. You may not realize this, but when you're dating, you look for a girl who has qualities that you're lacking in your own personality. At some point, you finally find someone with all of these qualities, and you fall in love. You get married, and it isn't long before you discover the reason that you *don't* have those qualities in your own life—you can't stand them! Now, your task for the rest of your life is to learn how to adapt to, and deal with, those qualities."

That was a real eye-opener. *Hmmm,* I thought. *God's going to have to provide a lot of help to me.*

But of course that's what He's in the business of doing. He's always there to give us His power to work out any and every problem. And it must have worked for us, because we've been married a long time now. (No, I'm not telling you how long!)

Seriously, if you're reading this and are thinking about marriage and seeking the perfect mate, I'd like offer you some advice that will save you a lot of heartache. Here it is:

Pray, pray, pray. Then wait, wait, wait.

What do I mean? I mean that God has the perfect person for you. He knows right where he or she is on Planet Earth. Pray that He will guide you to that person—and then wait on the Lord to deliver. He wants you happy today as well as forever.

This isn't a pie-in-the-sky idea. It's tried and true. I've seen the results in the lives of many people who've followed this formula—and it works beautifully, each and every time.

Maybe you're already married and are having troubles. I know it's tough—but this is a world of problems, and God is able to help you. Remember Don and April? A time came when they allowed the deceiver to get such a foothold in their lives that, after many years of marriage, they divorced.

But this story has a happy ending—because after much soul-searching, aided by counseling, they gave it all to God, and now, remarried, they are the happiest couple you'd ever want to meet. They've discovered that a successful marriage is a triangle—with God at the pinnacle. This "team of three" can conquer any evil lurking in a marriage.

But the devil wasn't done with Janene and me yet. We were about to go through an unbelievably faith-testing trial which almost jarred us loose from our church.

CHAPTER 14:

A REAL SHOCKER

We just didn't see it coming.

For about two years we owned a small home we'd built. It was just over a thousand square feet in size—not big, but nice. Then a contractor, whose father was best friends with our church elder, moved to town. Once we got acquainted, our conversation drifted into homebuilding. I told him about our house.

"Know what, Jim?" he said. "I can build you a new home more than twice the size, cheap. As a matter of fact, I can build you a brand-new home for about the same amount your present house would sell for. Are you interested?"

"It's a no-brainer," I told Janene later. "A new home, twice the size, for no additional money!"

"And he's a Christian too," she said. "And I know the head elder thinks he's trustworthy."

"Let's go for it," I said.

Janene: I had grown up living in the same home since I was 4 years old. Jim's parents had bought homes and fixed them up and then sold them for a profit, so he had moved so many times I think he lost count.

So when we built our first home, I was ready to stay there for the rest of my life—that is, until the opportunity came to have three times the home on three times the land for the same amount of money that our current home was worth! It sounded too good to be true, but I was really excited—and totally ready for all the sacrifice it was going to take to get there.

Jim: We put our little home up for sale, and soon the money was in hand—in the hand of the contractor, that is. . . .

But let me cut to the chase. This is too painful.

"Mr. Ayer?" An officer from the local bank was on the phone.

"Yes?"

"We need to talk to your contractor. Is he available?"

"What about?"

"He defaulted on his vehicle," said the officer. "And we're going to take his car back, as soon as we can find it."

Hmmm, I thought. *Seems kind of a strange way for a Christian to behave.*

I began to hear other things too—like one of our church members who was working on our new house who commented to me that when he'd gone to this contractor's truck to get a tool, he'd discovered a stack of *Playboy* magazines.

Finally after hearing a whole lot more that really disturbed me, I figured that as a Christian brother I should go talk to our contractor. We had a lengthy discussion, but he ended up blowing everything off as though it were nothing. Now all my money was gone—and our house was only partially completed. I brought this up with the church board, but they thought it was all my problem, because the head elder spoke so highly of his family. It was as if our local church leaders were blinded to everything.

Suddenly my "contractor"—and I use quotation marks because we discovered he wasn't really a contractor at all—had to leave town because the police were coming to get him for child molestation. He did end up going to prison—*but our church family still didn't believe Janene's and my side of the story, because this man's father was such good friends with certain church members. Therefore everybody believed that Jim and Janene were simply young and foolish.*

Janene: The problems which came up between us and our congregation really made me wonder what kind of a church we were part of. In the end, what it came down to was that I really had to consider my relationship with God. "God," I finally told Him, "it's *You* I'm going to church to be with, not people."

Since then I've learned that it's this kind of tragedy which chases a lot of people from our church today. *Don't let those who hurt you win!* If you do, you're playing right into the hands of the devil, who will do absolutely anything he can to take your eyes off Jesus.

Jim: The reason Janene and I are sharing this story with you is because nothing that ever happens to you—especially in your church—should cause you to leave the fellowship of God's people.

Remember the Matthew 15 story about the Canaanite woman with the demon-possessed daughter? Jesus evidently goes way out of His way to come to her town. She seems to have heard that He was the most powerful healer anybody had ever seen, so she tracks Him down.

"Have mercy on me, O Lord, Son of David!" she cries. "My daughter is severely demon-possessed!"

But Jesus doesn't say anything. It seems as though He has looked into the woman's heart, and has decided to make this a teaching moment. But His disciples are misreading His silence, and assume that He's just as prejudiced as they are.

"Send her away," they tell Jesus contemptuously. "She keeps crying after us."

Here's a poor woman desiring to draw near to Christ, and the 12 top church leaders say, "Get rid of her. She's bothering us. She's not worth the time."

Jesus breaks into their cutting comments. "I wasn't sent to anyone except to the house of Israel," He says thoughtfully.

The woman, listening, watches Jesus closely, and decides to try once more. She throws herself at His feet. "Lord, help me!"

Again, Jesus speaks thoughtfully, parroting Jewish prejudice against "unclean" heathens. And was there just a hint of humor in His tone, an "It's going to be all right" wink in His eye? "It's not good," He murmurs, "to take the children's bread and throw it to the dogs."

And you can hear the disciples' growls in the background. "Yeah. Amen. *Amen!*"

Now here's this woman, verbally abused by a pack of General Conference vice presidents, and on top of that, Jesus calls her a dog! But she catches on. Either that, or she's decided that absolutely nothing is going to keep her away from Jesus, no matter what.

Notice her quick-witted response.

"Yes, Lord," she says meekly. "Yet even the little dogs eat the crumbs which fall from their master's table."

Jesus can't play the game any longer. "O woman," He says fervently, anger at His disciples' prejudice mixed with admiration and love for her, "great is your faith! Let it be to you as you desire!"

And in a distant hut, a little girl convulses briefly, then sits up and looks around with wide, wondering eyes.

Dear reader, the deceiver is in the business of cutting off your communication with God. He would love nothing better than to have you leave the fellowship of believers, and thereby leave the side of Christ. He will give you a hundred seemingly justifiable reasons to depart, but *never, never, never go*. Gather strength from this woman's tenacity in the face of church rejection. Then resolve never to leave, no matter what.

Our experience with the "contractor" and the church was a terrible ordeal, but Janene and I survived. And eventually the full truth came out. We went to the bank and explained our problem, and they allowed us to borrow the money we needed to complete our home.

And guess whom we got to be the new contractor? Me! I experienced my first foray into the world of the owner-builder, and I gained a lot of good experience. However, I feel one deep regret, which still bothers me to this day. As general contractor, it was my job to call for the county inspector to come on a regular basis so that he could certify our work. This man usually showed up late, or not at all, and it soon became clear that he had a drinking problem.

Maybe I should talk with him about this, I thought. *Maybe there's some appropriate way to share Christ with him.*

But I felt a little uneasy. My stomach was full of butterflies, my mind was racing here and there, and I felt uncomfortable. I'd given a lot of Bible studies, and shared my testimony many times, but this time I just couldn't do it. I don't know why—maybe I was listening to the devil.

A few weeks later, I finally screwed up the courage. *I'll definitely talk to him at the next inspection,* I decided.

On the appointed day, I waited in anticipation, but he didn't show . . . and didn't show. Early that morning he'd been killed in a car crash. He'd been drinking, and that was his last day on earth. And I had missed the opportunity to share with him the perfect solution to all of his problems. Please, don't miss your opportunity to share the love of God with those who desperately need it.

Finally, after a grueling year both mentally and physically, we were in our new home. One evening at dinnertime, Janene started mixing a one-gallon glass jug of frozen orange juice. But it wasn't mixing very well.

"Let me help you with that," I said, like the sweet husband I am (it's true most of the time). I took the heavy jug in both hands and began to shake it rapidly. *Crash!* It slipped from my hands and fell into our brand-new porcelain sink, breaking into dozens of pieces. And under the mixture of gooey orange juice and broken glass was a large, black, serrated chip in the bottom of the sink.

"Oh, no!" we cried out in unison. It was the last straw. Floods of tears filled our eyes as we collapsed in one another's arms, sobbing heartbrokenly. But mixed with the sorrow over that really minor bit of damage were tears of weariness and tears of happiness. It had been a long, hard year, but our Lord had led us through the sea, vanquished our enemies who were in hot pursuit, and brought us to dry ground.

Janene: Finally we were in our new home. Wow, it was so nice! We had the most awesome view of Mount Shasta, a 14,162 foot snow-covered volcano.

Three stories, decks, three acres of land, and a large dog kennel. (I wanted to raise puppies and quit work at the phone company.) Our master bedroom had its own fireplace. The walls were lavender, the carpet a deep purple, and a large sliding door opened onto a deck that looked out at our majestic mountain. It was very romantic.

One night Jim and I were having one of our long, deep conversations. He was holding me in his arms. Suddenly he said soberly, "I have something to tell you. And it's really hard for me to get it out."

My heart went to my stomach. I was in a cold sweat. *What now? What can it be? He's so serious.*

"Honey," he said, "I used to have a girlfriend before I really knew you."

I remembered her. Her name was Sandi, and Jim had dated her when he was attending college. I knew he'd cared deeply for her, and that she had basically dumped him.

"After she left me and married another guy," he continued, "she had a little boy. I really believe he might be my son." Then he waited in silence, very concerned about what I was going to say.

My very first words were, "We need to find out. He needs to be a part of this family. You have to find out right away—and if he's yours, you need to be a part of his life."

"I *have* been trying to find out," he said, "but Sandi keeps telling me, 'He's not yours!'"

But Jim wanted me to know, because he felt for sure that the boy, whose name was Dan, was his son. I felt so bad for him, but I didn't know what to do. When our children, Jason and Meriah, were older we told them that they probably had an older brother but that he didn't know about them or their dad. But we wouldn't know the truth until much, much later.

CHAPTER 15:

FORK IN THE ROAD

Jim: Meanwhile, I was devouring the Bible and an increasing number of Ellen White's writings. One day I came across an interesting statement:

"Wherever there are a few Sabbathkeepers, the parents should unite in providing a place for a day school where their children and youth can be instructed. They should employ a Christian teacher, who, as a consecrated missionary, shall educate the children in such a way as to lead them to become missionaries" (*Advocate,* June 1, 1902).

We have "a few Sabbathkeepers" in our church, I thought. *So therefore, we need a school. True, we don't have any school-age children, but that's no problem for the Lord.*

I presented the idea to the church board. After reading the above quote, I told them, "If God said through His prophet that we should have a school, we should have a school."

Everyone said, "OK." Nobody said, "But where are we going to get some children?"

We decided to use one of the rooms in the church, and along with a couple of helpers—including Don Barnt—we soon had the room almost ready. But six weeks before school was to start, not only did we have no students, we had no teacher.

That's God's problem, I said to myself, *and there's no need to worry.*

A few days later I got a phone call. "Mr. Ayer?" said a female voice, "I understand you're looking for a teacher. I'm a teacher and would like to know more."

I invited her to come to the school, where I interviewed her and hired her on the spot. Then I called the conference and let them know. If that sounds backward to you, it is—but in those days our conference took a more relaxed approach, and I had built up a favorable track record with them. They said OK, and we had our new teacher.

Still no students, but that was God's problem.

A couple of weeks before opening day, two Adventist families moved to our area. And between them they had six children—all school-age! God is good! And the following year more families moved to the area, and our school continued to grow.

Meanwhile Janene and I, along with Don and April, had formed a singing-and-preaching witnessing team called Maranatha. We had a wonderful time bringing comfort to families whose children were into drugs and alcohol just as we had been. As they heard about the changes in our lives through the mighty miracles God had performed in us, they gained courage that if God could change us, He could change anybody—even their kids.

The conference started to call me to preach for vacationing pastors and for churches who were between pastors.

"Jim," Don told me, "you and I should go on the road as full-time evangelists."

"I'd love to," I said wistfully. "But you don't have any college, and I never finished my degree. Besides, once we get through school, they'll make us be pastors for a while before we can become evangelists."

Once I'd attended a ministerial meeting where the conference ministerial director told us, "Brothers, we are no longer fishers of men—we have become keepers of aquariums."

I wanted to *fish!* I didn't want to take care of any more aquariums—I already had a lot of those at Jungle Jim's. And if I was going to get into evangelism, I had to hurry up. I was 28 years old.

Finally, the urge and the call became so overwhelming that it was all I could talk about with Janene. Don and April had already sold almost everything they owned, enrolled in the Union College theology program, and loaded up their truck and headed to Lincoln, Nebraska.

It's time for us to do that too, we decided. *We need to sell everything and go back to school just like they have.*

We placed an ad in area papers, offering both the business and our home for sale. After one deal fell through on the advice of our tax advisor, an Adventist man called us.

"I want to buy everything," he said, "your home and your business. And as a down payment, I'll give a first trust deed as security on my apartment complex near Pacific Union College."

"This is exciting!" I told him. We did the paperwork, and I handed over the keys to everything we owned. Escrow had not yet closed, but I figured that would be a minor detail. We loaded up a rental truck and our two children (God had added a wonderful little girl named Meriah Dawn to our family), and were off to Pacific Union College in Angwin, California.

Janene: When we went to school, I sold my horse that I'd purchased right after Jerry died. That horse had gotten me through one of the hardest times in my life. The money was not important—I just wanted him to go to a good home. So I decided to donate that amount to a worthy cause (I can't remember what it is now) for God's ministry.

Let me jump ahead for a moment. When we came back from school, we didn't have a lot of money left. But my love for horses was burning deeply, and I just started looking around. My lifelong friend, Gail, had moved back to the area. She'd named her daughter Mariah (with an *a* where our girl's name had an *e*), because we assumed we would never live so close to each other that they'd have problems having the same names. (Both girls, however, grew up together and are good friends to this day.) Gail had property and horses, so she helped keep my horse-love alive.

I had always wanted to have a mare so that I could raise a foal, and I'd always loved Morgans. In our town was a man who had a Morgan mare named Windswept Carla, with a 2-year-old colt. The mare had a leg injury and could not be ridden, but she was just what I had always dreamed about. He was asking $500 for her. But since she wasn't rideable, paying out cash like this didn't go over well with Jim.

Still, I'd go and visit that horse several times a week. One day I had a phone call from the owner.

"I'd like to give you Carla as a gift," she said. "Is that all right with you?"

"Wow!" I said, overwhelmed. "I'll ask Jim."

Jim wasn't that excited. "But what else are you going to want?" he asked suspiciously.

"Money for hay, and a stud service," I said.

"OK, but you can't ask for any more horses for three years."

"I promise."

"And make sure you get registration papers with her."

Jim: Within five months Janene had two horses, and a third one on the way. *Hmmm.*

Janene: So I called the owner back and asked her about papers, and she said that yes, they intended for me to have the papers with Windswept Carla. And that was the beginning of my company, R Dream Kumtru Morgans. Carla was our foundation mare, and she produced our foundation stallion RDK's Shilo, who has offspring all over the world. She lived to be 38 years young. Somewhere there is a saying that you cannot outgive the Lord. Thank you, God, for your blessings!

But that would be in the future, and now it was time for Jim to go to school. When he and I arrived with the kids at Pacific Union College, it was quite a change. Not only were we changing our total lifestyle, but moving from a 2,400 square-foot home to a tiny two-bedroom apartment made life really challenging.

And underneath all the day-to-day duties I was panicking about becoming a pastor's wife. Was I ready for that? I felt really unprepared.

I miss my family, my home, my mountains, I said to myself. *And it's hard to be around all these strange people. Jim makes friends in a heartbeat, but I am so different. It takes me a long time to make a friend, and even then I'm not too sure.*

Years later, I would learn the term "missionary up." It's another way of saying, "Take courage. Even though things look tough, they could always be worse." In those times of dark uncertainty I would "missionary up" and talk to God about my worries, asking for help and strength to get me through each day. But I was scared, very scared.

Jim: I was facing my own mix of excitement and challenge. On the one hand, my urge to work full-time for God was becoming real. But my first day of Greek class made it even more real—*nightmarishly* real. My eyes scanned the workbook as I listened to the teacher. Everything he was saying was Greek to me! I left class that day shaken, wondering if I'd totally blown it. It had been years since I'd been in college. But I prayed for help, and help arrived. Soon I was actually getting A's in Greek and in most of my other classes as well.

It was an interesting time to be on campus. Dr. Desmond Ford had arrived at about the same time from Australia. He was a powerful speaker, a charismatic man who had developed many new theological ideas, all of which he was prepared to share with the students and faculty.

Janene and I attended his Friday night lectures, responding to his preaching with hearty amens. Later in the evening we'd attend Dr. Erwin Gane's "fireside talks," and again we would respond with strong amens.

Then when we got home, we would talk about what we heard. Suddenly, we realized that each man was putting forth ideas that were diametrically opposed to the other's. And we were saying "Amen" to both men's presentations.

So I began to study the subjects of perfection and the sanctuary with more earnestness than I'd ever done before. I concluded that Dr. Ford's new theology was extremely dangerous. And sadly, I was not wrong. Our campus soon became a lightning rod for ideas which would threaten to rock the very foundations of Adventism.

If you'd like to understand perfection and sanctification from a very practical standpoint, then please read my book *He Shall Lift You Up* (Remnant Publications, 2008). You'll discover that God has power to change you day by day, and He's ready, willing, and very able to do so. Once you embark on this exciting journey, you'll wish you'd started long ago.

Then suddenly we heard disturbing news from back home.

"Mr. Ayer," a person from the title company told me on the phone, "I don't know if you're aware of this, but the apartments your buyer is using as security already have a first trust deed."

"Does that mean what I think it means?" I asked.

"Probably. It means that if your buyer ever stops paying on your business and your home, you will not be in a safe position."

"But he didn't tell us about this!" I exclaimed. "What do I have to do?"

"My advice is for you to come back here and reclaim those properties from him."

My face felt numb. *Here we go again,* I thought. *Once more I've been defrauded by a member of my beloved Adventist church.*

We had to go back home, temporarily, and reclaim our properties, which the buyer had full possession of. And he wouldn't surrender them until we brought in attorneys. But finally we had everything back in our possession.

I don't know if you've noticed it, but I haven't been talking much about my prayer and study habits in recent pages. That's because I had stopped praying and studying.

"Hey, wait," I can hear you say. "You were taking theology, weren't you? That's Bible study, isn't it?"

No, it's not—not in the truest sense of growing a relationship with God. There's an old saying that goes, "You can be so busy doing the work of God that you forget the God of the work." See the difference? It's all about a relationship, and keeping the lines of communication open between you and God. And I had let my lines collapse.

Tragically, I no longer had that connection when I received a phone call from the president of the Nevada-Utah Conference.

"Jim, I'd like to offer you the pastorate of the brand-new church in Truckee. What do you think?"

"I appreciate the opportunity," I told him after a moment's thought. "But no."

My greatest desire had been to work full-time for God, and now I had a call to do just that. Why did I say no? Because I would have been paid only a stipend to start with, and I had a wife and two children to look after. So rather than keep my eyes upon the bigness of my God, I took my eyes off Him. I wasn't very different from the people God rescued from Egypt. He performed every mighty miracle He could for them, yet when it came time to enter the Promised Land, all they could see were the giants.

Janene: I look at it very differently. I don't think I was ready to be a pastor's wife. Just think about the great pastors you've known—and if you look carefully at their ministry, you find they have really great wives. I was very insecure at that point, and a pastor needs a really emotionally strong and powerful wife.

And I too had a hard time with the stipend. It would have been very small and insignificant. I did not see how we would exist. Maybe it was a lack of faith on my part—or maybe it was a mother's legitimate desire to protect her young. As I look back now, I see where God has led us, and I see the growth that took place in our lives—so I question Jim in his thinking that he let God down. I surely do wish God would just come down and talk things over with us. It would make it all so much easier!

Jim: I can understand why Janene feels the way she does. But I think I had lost the ability to listen to the "still small voice," the ability to see things through the eyes of God. I still wanted to attend school but the real reason to do so was missing—the burning desire had been exchanged for wanting to belong to the "fraternity of pastors" and now we were stuck at home again. I lost the trust in the One who is fully trustworthy. So now I began to stifle the voice that continued to call me back. Like Jonah, I began to run in the opposite direction.

And I don't think it's too dramatic to say of myself at that point, "I once was found—but now I'm lost."

CHAPTER 16:

LOST AGAIN

Once we were settled in back home in Mount Shasta, I was back at the store, hard at work. But one day I got a visit from Richard, a real estate broker I knew.

"Jim," he said, "I'm leaving the office I've been working out of, and I'm going to open my own. Would you like to join me?"

I didn't even have to think about it. "Yes," I said.

So Janene continued to run Jungle Jim's, and I put all my energy into becoming a successful real estate agent. It was slow going at first but I loved the challenge. I worked even harder, and tried to think up some creative advertising methods. Before too long I began to rise to the top of the business, and the money started flowing in. Richard and I expanded to bidding on tax sale properties and other types of properties, too.

Then Janene and I became silent partners in a Radio Shack business, and she began a small lamp manufacturing company, creating custom Victorian lampshades that were distributed through a large wholesale company. They sold the lampshades to the restaurant chain known as The Old Spaghetti Factory as well as other independent outlets. And we didn't forget Janene's desire to raise dogs, either—at one time or another we were raising and selling Siberian huskies, cocker spaniels, Kerry blue terriers, and bassett hounds.

Real estate suited me—one year I made more than 60 sales and had more than 100 active listings. I'd stopped advertising in the local real estate publications, and created, published, and distributed my own magazine. I was in the top 4 percent of the Coldwell Banker agents in North America. Money was no longer a problem for us. I even began day trading in the stock market.

Oh, I was still a church member, attending regularly and even preaching once in a while in my own church and in others. But my sermons weren't really spiritual—they were the kind of talks that Zig Ziegler or Tony Perkins might deliver: how to think positively, how to become a better person, and so on. I had emptied myself of the power of the Holy Spirit, and I'm sure people who were experiencing His presence could spot this instantly.

Janene and I were having fun—and fun was the name of the game. I loved every kind of sport: snow skiing, racquetball, scuba diving. I played in three baseball leagues. I conquered my fear of heights with rock climbing. I started riding a motorcycle again, bought a Harley, and built up the engine until that bike really screamed. I even let my hair grow into a little ponytail.

And God drifted further and further from my mind. I got into martial arts. Richard and I started a Chuck Norris United Fighting Arts Federation martial arts school, and when a kung fu master came to town, I became one of his first students. Eventually I earned a second degree black belt in kung fu san soo.

Sound fun? Of course it sounds fun. Because it *is* fun. All of it was. But these were also the actions of a man who had once heard the Voice, but who was now trying desperately to fill his God-void with everything but the One who really fills it.

I became the president of an organization called Save Our Skiing (SOS). Its purpose was to push forward a downhill ski development which had been approved by the Sierra Club and other environmental organizations, but whose construction had been halted. Later, I presided over KARE (Klamath Alliance for Resources and Environment), which won a national award for being the most active grassroots organization in the western United States. That meant that I was soon rubbing shoulders with United States congressmen and senators, and even the U.S. vice president. I was called before Congress as an expert witness on the renewal of the Endangered Species Act.

I started my own radio talk show called—what else?—"The Jim Ayer Show." I wrote op-eds for a newspaper and was regularly on the evening news, becoming a whiz at the 10-second sound bite.

And there was no room for God in what I was doing.

I had the same "I" problem—which is also an eye problem—the same problem the Laodicean church has. If I'd met an early death, the following quote from Revelation 3:17 could have been chiseled into my tombstone: *I am rich, and increased with goods, and have need of nothing.*

I knew the whole verse, of course. But because of my eye problem I couldn't apply it to me: Jesus says to the Laodicean church, *"You say, 'I am rich, have become wealthy, and have need of nothing'—and do not know that you are wretched, miserable, poor, blind, and naked."* Instead, I was already planning for an early retirement.

"Janene," I said one day, "let's sell everything and move down to Costa Rica. We could live like a king and queen there. You could have your own maid, and we could have a gardener and a cook and servants, and live in the lap of luxury for the rest of our lives."

Problem. You remember, don't you, how much Janene loves to move?

Janene: Once Jim completed a project and attained a goal, the fun and challenge were gone, and it was time to look for the next big challenge. It had been this way our entire marriage. Now he wanted to move to Costa Rica—and I didn't want to leave our parents. I had already lost my mom to ovarian cancer and since I was an only child, my dad had only me.

Jim's parents were getting older, and since he was an only child, they had only us. And I didn't want to leave our children and my horses. I was hoping he would find something close by to focus his energy on.

Well, there is something I have learned over the years. If you don't want something, don't ask God for it. Because if God decides it's what's your life needs, then you are going to get it. And I got it sooner than I ever dreamed.

Jim: One Sabbath morning I was sitting in church, when the Voice spoke to me. It was the same Voice that had spoken to me many years before.

Jim.

I blinked. "What?"

Jim, the Holy Spirit may be falling all around you, but you will not recognize it or receive it.

This shook me to the core. *I don't want to be lost,* I remember thinking frantically, *but I know right now that if the Lord returns today, no matter how good I look and how much I support the church or how successful I am, I am lost!* Guilt washed over me as I looked back over wasted years, years when I was ignoring God's leading while pretending I was a wonderful Christian.

Lucky for me, God is a God of second chances. I remembered Elijah's story. As a mighty man of God, he stood on Mount Carmel, fearlessly calling a nation and her king to repentance. He called down fire from heaven, killed all the prophets of Baal, and prayed rain back to a parched countryside.

But then his iron grasp upon the Almighty turned to Jell-O, as he fled from a solitary woman who spewed threatenings against God's man. He ran until he could run no longer. Finally he found himself at a cave far, far away. And as 1 Kings 19 tells it, in a still small voice God asked him a question: *What are you doing here?*

Elijah replied, trying to justify his running away, but God asked again: *What are you doing here?* And the prophet finally got it, and headed back "on mission." He'd taken grateful advantage of a loving God and His second chances.

"I've got to do something," I said to Dan, a friend of mine who was an orthopedic surgeon, as I told him a little of my experience.

"I've been feeling the same way," he replied. "Our lives are not what they should be."

So we decided on a plan of action. We would get a group of people together and meet on Friday nights and "do something."

Dan happened to mention our plan to his brother Joe, a dentist in Oregon.

"Have you heard of the book *Experiencing God*?" Joe asked. "It's authored by a couple of Southern Baptists, and I hear it's really good."

So Dan picked up some copies, and we gathered at his home Friday night with about 10 other people who also wanted more in their Christian experience—more of *something*, even though no one was sure what it might be. Dan, who was leading the group, began to talk us through the instructions.

"Now the first thing we have to do," he said, "even before we start this first session, is to turn to the back of the workbook and sign the covenant there. It says that you have to spend daily time in study and prayer seven days a week. The way the book sets it up, it will come to about 45 minutes a day."

All around me, people were quickly turning to the covenant and writing their signatures. *Oh, no,* I thought. as I read the instructions in the book. *How can I sign this? I'm too busy.* What I was really saying, of course, was, *How can an important person like me take that kind of time out of my life?*

I sat there with the notebook in my lap. I hadn't signed the covenant, but no one seemed to have noticed.

As the evening went along, I found myself in pain. Not physical pain, but mental pain. The still small voice of the Holy Spirit was working overtime on me, pressuring me to sign that covenant. But I kept digging in my heels.

Finally the meeting was nearly over. There was one more section of the study to complete—watching a 15-minute videotape by one of the book's authors, Dr. Henry Blackaby. And I felt like he was speaking directly to me. He said that even if God called me to go on a mission for Him, it would be impossible for me to respond, because I'd piled so much garbage in front of my door that I wouldn't be able to get to the door to answer the call. And it was true.

It's a good thing the lights were off, because the tears were trickling down my cheeks. God was speaking through that man directly to me, and He was hitting the mark. I had indeed piled up years of this world's garbage. I possessed everything that the world called success, but I had turned my back on God in the process, and was heading in the opposite direction. What could I do?

The video was over, and the lights were back on. Everyone was very moved by the meeting, and talked excitedly all the way to the front door. But I hung back, workbook in hand, still opened to the covenant page. Again, as had happened years before in that basketball-auditorium scene, the struggle between my God and the deceiver was powerful and very real. I had only moments to decide. I had again arrived at the crossroads of eternity. What was I going to do?

Chapter 17:

Second Chance

Well, when the Voice speaks to you—and it's spoken by One so incredibly patient as God—there's only one thing you can do. I took out my pen and wrote my name on the covenant line.

Floods of relief rolled over me. I had been lost, and found, and lost again. But God hadn't given up on me. He had given me a *Second Chance!* Praise God!

And from the moment I chose God again, life would never be the same.

Janene: Jim always had an easy time studying the Bible with anyone—except me. I think it was a husband-wife thing. When I asked him a spiritual question, he would hand me a book, or direct me to the *SDA Bible Commentary* and tell me that my answer was right there. I had come along with Jim to the *Experiencing God* study group, and I was excited about it. I couldn't sign that covenant fast enough, and couldn't figure out why Jim was taking so long.

As the weeks passed and our group progressed through this study, we grew much closer to God and to each other, closer than we could ever have imagined possible. We all still look back on that study time as a turning point in our walk with God.

Jim: Remember how one of my supposed problems was that I didn't have spare time to study and pray? What happened in the next few days was amazing to me—God impressed me to cancel all the premium channels in my TV package. That's right, no more filthy-language HBO channels or any other shows like that.

Along with that change, He spoke to Janene and me, asking us a question, *What is the most important thing in this world?* I can tell you now, it wasn't TV. Almost immediately He helped us both make a gigantic priority shift, and we were happy to do it.

It's like the story of the manna in the wilderness back in Exodus. Remember how God told the people to pick up the manna in the morning each day, and on Friday to gather double the amount?

That's like daily Bible study. Prayer and study are our spiritual food, and we can't get along on just one meal a week. We need to gather the heavenly food daily. And God told the people to gather manna early in the morning before it got too hot. Our study time should be early in the day before our schedule heats up. And finally, it was impossible for people to gather more manna than they needed for one day. You see, today's experience is no good for tomorrow. We need a fresh experience with God every day.

And it's like marriage, too. Couples who've been married for any length of time realize that if they don't talk to one another regularly they're going to have problems. It's no different when you're trying to maintain a relationship with God.

Right around this time I watched a video featuring Becky Tirabassi, a woman whose life was dramatically impacted by God. He led her to start a practice she called journaling. Before I learned to do this I would be praying—maybe while lying in bed—and my mind would start wandering all over the place. My mind is always going a hundred directions at once. Then I would catch myself and start praying again: "Lord, bless this food. Oh! I'm not eating. Sorry, Lord."

Maybe this journaling will help me focus, I thought. *I'll try it.*

Journaling is sort of like writing letters to God—pouring out your heart to Him. I was thrilled with the results. Before this, it had seemed hard for me to pray even for 10 minutes, but as I tried this exciting way of talking with God, I could go easily for an hour or more.

Don't get me wrong. I'm not saying that you or anybody else should do this for the sake of clicking time off the clock. I'm saying that it becomes such a wonderful and powerful communication tool that soon you're spending time with God because you're in love with Him and He is your best Friend.

The neat thing was that not only Janene and I, but our entire Friday night study group, were growing spiritually by leaps and bounds. We couldn't wait to get together each week to talk about God. Interesting, isn't it? I went from no-time to full-time. But after all, the Bible speaks of the Holy Spirit as a "tongue of fire," and when God is in you, you are on fire.

But there were still some hurdles.

One Sabbath I was sitting in church listening to the sermon, and my mind drifted far off in another direction—to Costa Rica. (Remember? Servants, gardeners, maids? Living in the lap of luxury?) Maybe Janene and I could make a trip down there this summer and check out real estate prices, I wondered. That would give us a chance to see how we liked it. And maybe we could also—

Jim, said the Voice.

My skin prickled. I waited.

Jim, you need to do something for Me this year.

Let me stop for a moment and say a couple of words about the "voice" thing. I hope you've figured out by now that this is not a book on how you can hear the specific Voice that I have heard. God speaks to people in many different ways—sometimes through trusted friends, sometimes through Scripture, sometimes through nagging feelings that won't go away. Think about it. How many times did He speak to people through a burning bush? Just once. How many times did he use a donkey to speak to someone? Just once. Or remember Paul in the blinding light? That's the only recorded time God spoke to anyone in that manner. He tailors His method of communication to each person's personality.

But make no mistake, He does speak to us. "My sheep," He said, "hear my voice, and they follow me." He chooses the best method—burning bush, talking donkey, trials, tribulations—and He lovingly waits for you and me to say yes.

Church was over. The organ was playing something majestic as we walked slowly to the foyer. After the usual handshaking and goodbyes, Janene and I headed to the car.

"Honey," I told her, "God just let me know that we needed to do something for Him this year."

She didn't miss a beat. "Let's go on a Maranatha trip," she said.

My mouth dropped open. *Is this my Janene talking, my sweetheart who doesn't like to leave her home and her kids and her horses, doesn't like to go on impulsive adventures?*

And she also hadn't said, "How do you know it was God talking?" She and I have learned that as you walk with the Lord, certain things become evident. And to both of us, this was natural, because at that point we were committing our lives to the Lord moment by moment, and therefore we could more easily recognize His moving in our lives.

Janene: That morning when I was getting ready for church, I too had been impressed with doing something for God. The times God speaks to me are when I am having a quiet time by myself. And this impression was so exciting, because it was something Jim and I had talked about doing many years before. And now seemed like the right time—especially when Jim suddenly brought it up on the way home from church.

Jim: On Monday I called the Maranatha office. (Maranatha Volunteers International is a wonderful organization which builds churches, schools, orphanages, and other buildings as needed, anywhere and everywhere in the world.) "Where are you working right now?" I asked them. "My wife and I would like to join you on a trip."

"Right now we have projects in Irian Jaya and Central America," they said.

We picked the trip which had the cheapest airfare (just because you make a lot of money doesn't mean you need to spend it all!), and began packing our bags for a place we've never heard of before: Barquisimeto, Venezuela.

When we arrived, we found that a tent city had been set up which could house a construction team of 180 people. Eight churches and two large gymnasium school projects were on the drawing board. Our roommates for the next two weeks were a sweet, elderly, and apparently quite tottery, couple from Canada.

"These people are going to help *build*?" Janene whispered to me after we met them.

"I was thinking the same thing," I said. "They can hardly move."

That first night we also learned that our tentmates snored—snored so loudly that the tent was almost shaking. Each night thereafter, Janene and I got to bed as soon as we could, earplugs firmly in place.

I was stunned to discover that once he hit the worksite, the shuffling, bent-over man immediately became at least as powerful as his snoring. Every day he mixed mortar to fill cement blocks, which meant that he lifted five-gallon buckets of mortar up over his head, again and again. Can you imagine how much those buckets must have weighed? He did that all day long, at a very fast pace! And the minute he got back to camp, he again became a shuffling, bent-over, kindly old man. And we found that God provided strength to everyone in the camp, regardless of age, including us.

I still remember something that happened on my first days laying cement block for the Venezuelan church wall. Another Maranatha volunteer across from me glanced over at some of the local people who were helping us.

"You know, Jim," he said thoughtfully. "Isn't it wonderful that we are the answer to the prayers of so many people?"

It hit me! *I'm an answer to prayer!* I couldn't remember ever having been an answer to anyone's prayers. A rush of feelings flowed over me as I realized that I was smack-dab in the center of God's will for my life.

Janene, who was working in the kitchen, experienced the same revelation. Each evening as we met in our tent, we were exhausted and excited at the same time. We couldn't wait to talk about the events of the day—and we decided that as soon as we got home we were going to visit the Maranatha office in

Sacramento and see if there was a project we could organize. We were hooked.

And then we quickly prayed together, and jumped into bed before the snoring started.

From the *Experiencing God* book we learned that God is always at work—and when He reveals where He is working, that becomes our invitation to join Him. It was so exciting to see the hand of God orchestrating our lives.

Back home, we hit the ground running. The island of Dominica needed a school complex completed in time for classes to begin, and that meant we had to have a team of at least 30 people ready to go within a month—a very tall order. We didn't know anybody who might be willing to go with us—but within the month we were on our way to the Caribbean with a team of 32 people who had come from all over California and beyond. We serve a God who specializes in tall orders, and nothing is impossible for Him.

I remember two thrilling highlights from the Dominica trip. The first was driving on the left-hand side of the road. The second was being able to preach again. Wow, did that feel good! What a difference it is to preach when you have the Holy Spirit, as opposed to winging it without God's blessing or power.

Back home, we rang up Maranatha. "We're ready to lead another team!"

"How about Honduras?" they suggested. "You'll be constructing a church."

"Sign us up," we said promptly.

But this trip would be dramatically different. One evening a few days before our departure I was watching CNN. "Janene!" I shouted from the living room, my eyes glued to the TV. "Come look at this!"

The screen was filled with images of lashing palm trees and driving rain. Hurricane Mitch had just slammed into Honduras.

Chapter 18:

A Drug Dealer Again

I shook my head in disbelief. "Janene, how can we take our team there? There'll be no chance of getting clean water, and the food is going to be suspect too."

"And think of all those injured people," Janene said.

"Right. So we'd have to add a medical team along with everything else."

With only a few phone calls I found me a company that provided low-cost drugs for medical supplies. *Jim Ayer, drug dealer,* I thought wryly. *But at least this time, I'm dealing for God.* The medical team came together with providential swiftness, and now we were ready to build a church, do a short evangelistic series, and even provide some medical help.

Our arrival at the airport could've been a scene in an action movie—a comedy action movie. With minutes to make it to the checkout counter, dozens of people scrambled to unload more than 5,000 pounds of gear from the bus. But no matter how many times we counted and recounted, we simply had too many bags and far too much weight to get on the plane.

"What are we going to do?" one of the team asked.

"God will need to take care of it," I said. In those bags was medicine for thousands of people, food for dozens of team members, and even gifts for little children—all vital supplies.

Lord, we prayed, *we are placing this matter in Your hands, and we are going to leave the results with You. We are on Your mission, so this is Your problem.*

I approached the ticket counter and plopped a huge pile of passports in front of the female agent. Then, with solid trust—well, *almost* solid—in the Lord, I pointed toward our mountain of army duffel bags waiting to be piled on the scales.

What happened next was a miracle. She simply motioned for the team to stack them up.

I stared at her.

Again, she silently jerked her thumb in a *Get these things on the conveyor belt* kind of motion. No checking the scales, and no bag count! So one by one, those precious supplies disappeared through the little door in the wall, bound for Honduras.

My shoulders were starting to relax, and the butterflies had stopped doing their Cossack clog-dance in my tummy. I led our group to the gate we'd be departing from, when suddenly we saw a grim-lipped airport official approaching.

"I'm looking for a Jim Ayer," he said.

"Right here," I said. "What can I do for you?"

"Come with me."

He led me down some stairs and all the way back into the bowels of the airport complex. This was long before the days of heavy airport security. *What's going on?* I wondered.

We eventually arrived in a small holding area where one of our bags sat alone on the floor. Out through a tiny hole it its side was pouring grains of a fine white powder.

"What is that powder?" the official demanded.

I began to laugh. *They're thinking it's cocaine or heroin,* I decided. "It's powdered milk," I said. And, of course, it was.

During the next few weeks we touched the hearts of thousands of people as we treated more than 3,200 medical patients, shared the gospel with many, and constructed a beautiful house of worship.

But the people who were touched the most were *us*. We learned—as we have learned so many times since then—that when you go on a mission from God, you return a different person.

At this time Janene and I did not own any businesses but were self-employed, so we had no income except what we earned by selling real estate and lamps between mission trips. Years before, as our real estate work became more successful, we had sold everything in the Jungle Jim store and dissolved the business.

Prior to God speaking to us and turning us around, we had purchased rental properties and had a very large debt service to pay on each month. If we didn't work, we didn't make money. But no matter how many teams we put together, and no matter how often we went on those humanitarian and gospel-sharing trips, when we returned, the money came in to pay all of the bills.

We really began to understand Jesus' promise, "Therefore do not worry, saying, 'What shall we eat?' or 'What shall we drink?' or What shall we wear?' For after all these things the Gentiles seek. For your heavenly Father knows that you need all these things. But seek first the kingdom of God and His righteousness, and all these things shall be added to you" (Matt. 6:31-33).

I don't know how God does it. It makes my head spin to try to imagine how He can mesh huge bills with a reduced income stream and tie everything off to keep the debt collectors from knocking at the door. But that's why He is God and I am not. You and I are only asked to "seek first the kingdom of God and His righteousness."

And it's fun to watch other people discover this too.

"Randy," I said to a friend of mine. "Come with us on our next trip. We need your dental expertise."

"But I've never gone on one of these things before," he said. "And I can't leave my practice."

"Why not?"

"Do the math," he said. "I need to keep generating income so I can pay my staff and keep ahead of all my costs. I wouldn't be able to afford it."

"Randy," I said patiently, "if God calls you to go, you can't afford *not* to go. Why don't you pray about this? You've got some time—the trip won't be for several months"

"OK," he said doubtfully.

Two months later, our phone rang.

"Jim," Randy said, "I've been praying about this trip, and it does seem that God wants me to go along."

"Great!" I said. "We'll plan on it then. I know you'll be blessed."

Two more months, and the phone rang again.

"Jim!" Randy could hardly control his excitement. "You'll never guess what's happened. In the last two months my dental office has done *six* months worth of business! I've never had anything like this happen before. That means I have enough money to keep all my staff on payroll while we're gone, and also to pay off all my bills."

I grinned as I hung up the phone and pondered what I'd just heard. *I used to believe it was fun to turn people on to drugs,* I thought. *Turning people on to mission trips is a thousand times more thrilling.* Randy's call was exciting, but not unexpected. Janene and I were getting used to anticipating great things now that we'd allowed God to take the driver's seat.

So nowadays when I hear someone say, "I don't have the money to go on a mission trip," that's simply not an excuse I can accept. "If God wants you to go," I respond, "He will provide the money. He owns the cattle on a thousand hills, and all He has to do is sell a few of those cows to support your trip. What you need to do is make certain that you are in the center of His will for your life." After escorting hundreds and hundreds of people on mission trips around the world, I have yet to see a time when God did not take care of those He has asked to go for Him.

Costa Rica was Maranatha's next "construction target country." Dozens of churches and schools needed to be built by short-term mission volunteers.

"Do you know what we need?" I said to the Costa Rican church leaders and Maranatha officials. "We need a paid Bible worker labor force. That way, these Bible workers can be preparing people for baptism six months in advance of a building project. And when the Maranatha team arrives, they can not only build a church but hold an evangelistic series, and have 20 to 60 people baptized that weekend."

The people I talked to were delighted. Maranatha began advertising this great opportunity so teams could budget Bible worker stipends. It was a great joy, on dedication Sabbaths, for these teams to experience dozens of baptisms.

And Janene and I finally made it to Costa Rica—not to retire and live in the lap of luxury, but to work with 52 volunteers from all over the United States and other countries.

But the Costa Rica trip would give us an adventure we hadn't planned on.

Getting to one of our sites wasn't easy. I had to hire several wooden dugout canoes to ferry our medical-dental team up an alligator-infested river running along the Panamanian border. But the smiles we saw when we finally arrived at the distant jungle village were ample payment for our dicey journey and well worth the time we labored there.

And work was just as fun at site number 2—even when I slid off a roof and ripped open my finger on a large protruding screw. That night, everybody enjoyed gathering around a tiny lamp in the storage shed to watch a team doctor stitch up my finger using dental Novocain to ease the pain.

(Oh, and speaking of Novocain. I forgot to mention that, after taking so many medical and dental teams on mission trips, I learned how to clean teeth and even extract them. Yup, yours truly, who'd been afraid of dentists and their offices all his life, has become something of a practicing developing-world dentist! And Janene has become a very good developing-world dental assistant and pharmacist.)

With our work in the villages completed, I figured everyone had earned a little time off to relax and visit the countryside. My plan was to take a van full of people to a beach 10 miles away to watch gigantic turtles lay their eggs. I'd hired a guide to meet us at our destination.

We started a little before dark. We'd been having torrential rains for several days, but the weather was clearing up and the temperature was very comfortable. On a scouting trip several months back, I had checked out the route. But that evening, everything looked different, mainly because there was raging water everywhere. Even though the tropical rains had ceased, the waters were still pouring down from high mountain slopes.

"OK," I said, as our van paused at a certain point. "This is where the bridge is *supposed* to be. Right here."

However, the water had risen so high that I couldn't see any real evidence of a road or a bridge. Gripping the steering wheel tighter, I inched forward, water swirling around our 14-passenger van.

I began to speed up so I wouldn't stall in the water, which was getting deeper every minute. After a few white-knuckle moments, I recognized a landmark that told me that I was now safely on the other side. Everyone rejoiced as we hurried toward the beach, found our guide, and started hunting for the turtles.

"No turtles," I finally said to the guide. "Where are they?"

"I'm sure there are some across that river," he said, pointing ahead. "It's not too deep."

I gazed doubtfully at what I could see of the rain-swollen river in the darkness.

"I'll go across and see if I can find some," he suggested.

"OK," I told him, "we'll wait here."

Off he went, and we settled down on the beach. The temperature was delightful, and we were soon fast asleep.

Soon he was back. "I found some," he said. "Follow me."

By now it was so dark that we could remove most of our clothing, hold it above our heads, and wade into the chest-deep water. The current was really slow, and we had no problem getting across to the other side. And with our eyes adjusted to the darkness, we could see the turtles, God's wonderful huge creatures, laying dozens of large creamy eggs. We made it safely back across the river and into the van, and when we'd driven back to the "invisible bridge," the water had subsided so we could see it. We crossed it and came safely back to camp.

The next day I was telling some of the people in the village about our midnight adventure, crossing the bridge we couldn't see and then fording the swollen river in our skivvies. Their faces turned pale.

"You didn't cross *that* river, did you?"

"Sure we did," I said. "What's the problem?"

"That river is full of crocodiles!"

Praise the Lord for His protective angels.

Adventures followed thick and fast as we traveled across the globe. One of the most heart-wrenching of these began with another phone call from Maranatha.

"Jim, we could really use you to oversee an orphanage project in Bangladesh," said the Maranatha staffer.

"Sign us up," I said automatically. Janene and I were growing accustomed to saying yes to God's leading—but nothing could prepare us for what we would encounter in that very interesting land.

It turns out that some of the Bangladeshi gods are blond females, so when we arrived, Janene began to draw very large crowds of adoring males. These men thought nothing of encroaching upon her personal space, touching her hair, or staring endlessly at her from six inches away.

The orphanage and school complex housed 700 children, a staggering number of lovely, dark-eyed youngsters. As on our other mission trips, our hearts began to form powerful, loving bonds with these kids. But one in particular tugged at our heartstrings. Bithica was a pretty 9-year-old girl who'd been living at one of the teachers' homes because her parents could no longer afford to keep her with them.

The workday had ended, and I had returned to our living quarters to relax and gather around the dinner table with a few friends. Janene suddenly entered the room with a very unhappy look on her face.

I gave her a concerned glance. "What's the matter, honey?"

"It's Bithica."

"What's wrong?"

Janene's voice quavered. "She's going to be sold," she said.

"Sold! What do you mean?"

"Her tenth birthday is today," Janene replied with tears in her eyes. "And her parents are going to sell her as a slave. Either that or a prostitute."

Gasps sounded around our table. "But *why?*" I asked.

Janene gave a muffled sob. "They can't afford to keep her anymore. And they need the money."

We all sat silent, staggered by this completely foreign, completely devastating news. I began to pray silently. Suddenly, the silence was broken by one of our friends, who stared me straight in the eye.

"Why don't you buy her?" he asked.

Chapter 19:

One Miracle After Another

Janene and I stared at our friend, our jaws sagging. "Could we do such a thing?" she finally gasped.

"How would we go about it?" I asked. "And—what would she *cost*?" I just could not wrap my mind around this idea. *Jim Ayer, God's drug dealer* was one thing, but *Jim Ayer, God's slave dealer?*

"Somebody's got to do something," another friend said. "Can you imagine the fate of that sweet little girl if she's sold?"

Janene and I looked at each other. "We'll do it," she said.

I nodded, my face numb. "No matter what the cost, we'll buy Bithica."

Within a week, we had purchased our own little girl.

I know it sounds strange, especially in Western countries, to own someone. But with no negotiation on our part, we paid the grand total of $10 for Bithica. We placed her in school so she could receive a proper education and we also began helping her parents financially so that they would not be tempted to offer their four other children for sale.

I'll never think of the country of Nepal without remembering a mission trip we took there. One day we were at work, and two weary-looking nurses from the local hospital hurried into the camp.

"Can you help us?" they asked.

They told us a story no Hollywood scriptwriter could ever dream up. A Hindu farmer had given up on life. His wife was a drunkard, and his crops had failed, so he had decided to follow a local custom and commit suicide by taking poison. In that part of the world, many people come to the point where their money is gone and there is no hope left. Sometimes they will thoroughly poison the final meal so as to kill the entire family.

However, this farmer had two sons who loved him and didn't want him to die. When they found him writhing on the floor, they picked him up and carried him to the hospital. Just as he crossed the threshold, his lungs shut down. The nurses quickly placed a tube down his airway, and attached a hand-operated rubber bag which would inflate his lungs and breathe for him.

This was a mission hospital with no modern technology. By the time the two nurses came to us for help, they had "bagged" this fellow for 48 hours by hand to keep him alive, but now they had just run out of energy and there was no additional staff who could spare the time to help sustain this man's life.

"Can you help us?" they begged. "Can you please send some people to keep this man alive so that we can get some rest?"

There was, of course, only one answer to that question.

Several volunteers immediately stepped forward, and we began to arrange shifts. Mine wasn't until the following day and I was glad for that. I've told you how much I fear dentists, and if you can believe it, I have an even greater horror of hospitals. To me, a hospital is a place you go to die. I've heard that you can catch diseases in hospitals—and this would especially be true in the Third World, where ugly viruses lurk in every darkened corner, maladies that doctors in the U.S.A. only read about in textbooks.

I returned to my room that night and spent a long time with my head buried in my pillow, talking to God.

You know how I hate hospitals, Lord! I prayed. *Why did this have to happen? I would never let someone die because I refused to help—but how can I help when I am paralyzed with fear?*

After an hour or so, God gave me a wonderful peace which allowed me to fall sound asleep until the next morning. I got up and headed toward the rendezvous with the nurse and my Hindu farmer.

Light in the mission hospital was almost nonexistent. Patients spilled out into the halls, some lying between blood-stained sheets, others sitting on the edges of their dirty beds with tubes dangling precariously from various body parts. I finally negotiated my way to the dingy room where my patient was clinging to life.

My eyes quickly surveyed every corner. There was no equipment except a few miscellaneous items including a monitor that flickered from time to time as though it had a will of its own.

The nurse beside the bed looked at me with relief in her eyes. "You can watch the monitor," she said, "but it's not very accurate. You will do better if you watch his chest rise and fall." She gave me five minutes of hands-on instruction, showing me how to squeeze the blue bag attached to the clear tube that disappeared down his throat.

Then she said quickly, "Your shift will be half an hour. Then someone will come to relieve you. Goodbye." *Poof*, she was gone—and I was left alone with my Hindu farmer gazing up at me through his coal black eyes.

I wonder what your life was like before, I thought as I gazed back at him. *What are you thinking right now? Do you wonder who this stranger is, this foreigner who is providing you life with every flex of his already tiring muscles? He has your life in the palms of his hands.*

I found myself having to fight back waves of panic, but I was sustained by my Lord as I prayed for this fellow whose life was dependent upon every squeeze of the soft rubber bag. I was glad my shift would be just half an hour, because my hands were becoming very tired. I'm sure some of my fatigue was due to stress, but mostly it was because it was really hard work to compress that bag with just the right pressure, in just the right rhythm, without stopping. When my time was up, I was so relieved that I rushed out and gasped in all the fresh air I could, flexing my wrists to try to get the circulation back.

The next day I was back beside my new friend with the bag between my hands. He seemed more responsive to me than he'd been the day before, and this time I talked out loud to him.

"I'm sure you don't know what I am saying to you," I said, "but I want you to know that things are not as bad as they seem right now. There is a God who loves you, and wants to be your friend."

Oh, how I wish I had the gift of tongues, I thought as I placed one of my hands on his forehead, the other still pumping air. "God, thank you for my new friend," I prayed. "Please heal him. Draw him to You. In Jesus' name I ask this. Amen."

My half hour had passed, and the hour mark was rapidly approaching, but still no one came to relieve me. Two hours passed, and still no relief. But strangely, my hands were not getting tired. Then I noticed his chest seemed to be puffing up, everywhere! Suddenly his entire chest cavity expanded to twice its size.

What could I do? Anchored to my post, I began yelling for anyone to come and help. A nurse finally appeared at the door, glanced at the man, and in the next instant, doctors and nurses were everywhere, blood was flying, slits appeared in his chest wall, but no one said a word to me. I was in the middle of a real emergency room event, a bona fide team member, observing, but still providing life-giving air to my patient and friend.

Fifteen or 20 minutes passed, and as fast as they had appeared, the entire staff left the room, and I was once again alone with my Hindu farmer. Three hours passed, then three and a half, and still no one came to take my place. The man's dark eyes looked up at me with longing as I continued to talk to him, stroke his brow, and pray for him. During hour number 4, my replacement finally showed up. Over my entire four-hour ordeal, my hands had not become tired at all.

By the time we left for the States, my Hindu friend was able to hand-compress his own airbag and provide himself with oxygen when needed. Three weeks later I received a message from one of the hospital nurses. "He walked out of the hospital today under his own power," she reported. "He wanted to know who the people were who saved him, and who their God was, because he is going to attend their church."

By now, mission work had permeated Janene's and my entire DNA. If we weren't actually on a trip, we were planning the next one. We lived for those trips—and loved them. In my daily journaling I began to write, "Lord, help me reach the world for you!"

And God responded in ways that make my skin prickle when I think of them.

"Jim," said a caller one day. "I would like to sponsor an evangelistic series to India, and I would like you to organize it and preach it. What do you say?"

This was long before such meetings in India had become common, but Janene and I were always up for the exotic. It sounded too good to pass up. "We'll be glad to," we said. And soon we began to formulate plans and make contact with church leaders in Cuddapah, India.

In no time I had assembled a small team of seven people. Each of us had had mission experience, but none of us had ventured to India before. And none of us had any idea of what lay ahead. We knew it would be a challenge—but we didn't realize how big that challenge would be.

With bundles of cash strapped to our waists, bags packed to bursting, malaria pills stuffed into our carry-ons, and a 15-pound video projector in tow, we were prayed up, packed up, and ready to be picked up. We hopped onto Thai Airlines and hunkered down for the grueling flights. Twenty-four hours later we arrived in Chennai, India, where we loaded the gear into a couple of cars and headed north for eight more hours of hot, stinky travel.

We had no idea what to expect on opening night, but our excitement grew as we witnessed a sea of people pouring into the meeting area to hear the gospel message. Night by night, as word spread, the meetings grew larger and still larger. Some of our guests traveled two hours one way, standing packed like sardines in the back of gravel trucks, to hear us. In the years since, I've watched this scene repeat itself again and again—thousands of people braving long distances and storms to hear about the Creator God. Even when we had to turn off the power to the sound system because a chilling rain was coming down in torrents, the people sat listening to the message of hope found only in Jesus Christ. I was cold and miserable, and ready to go home, but how could I? I must tell them!

Finally the night came when I would be presenting the truth about the Sabbath. Before the meeting started, my translator, who pastored a large university church, approached me with a serious expression.

"Pastor Ayer," he said, "I just want to let you know that the devil will be extremely angry about what you say this evening."

Staring wide-eyed at him, I swallowed. "What do you think is going to happen?"

"Anything might happen," he said. "You must be prepared."

The meeting got underway. Though I had been very sick for several days, I was feeling better and felt in sync with my translator. I was preaching forcefully about God's great memorial day of Creation when all of a sudden loud cries rose from the section of the crowd on my right side. I ignored them and continued to preach.

But suddenly a woman approached the platform carrying a lifeless form in her arms, wailing with terrible grief. Her look of anguish told the story, and so did the figure of the boy in her arms. He lay motionless, eyes rolled back in his head, his arms hanging limply like a rag doll's.

I stopped and took a hard look. *Could he be . . . dead?*

Many people gathered around this woman, and as they came close to the boy, they uttered more ear-piercing cries of anguish.

I quickly beckoned to one of our team who was a medical doctor. He ushered the woman to the left side of the stage, and began to examine the child.

It's time to pray, Jim, I told myself, taking a deep breath. *And this is going to have to be a real rubber-meets-the-road prayer.*

I began to pray aloud into the microphone. "God, You are a big God, and I call upon You to answer our prayer of help. Send Your power to defeat the devil, so that You will be glorified before these people."

Chapter 20:

Casting Out Demons

As I continued to pray, every once in a while I would crack open an eye and glance to my left and see what the doctor was doing. Then I would close my eyes and pray more earnestly. After about the fifth or sixth "peek," I saw a smile on the doctor's face. He gave me a thumbs-up sign.

"Thank You, Almighty King of the universe!" I prayed into the microphone. "To you we give all the glory and praise! In Jesus' name. Amen."

I opened my eyes again and glanced down to the left. The mother was all smiles, and the boy was doing fine. The mourners had changed their sobs to screams of joy, and I finished preaching the Sabbath message to an absolutely spellbound audience.

To this day I still wonder if that boy was actually dead. Even my friend the doctor can't offer a clinical decision with 100 percent certainty. "All I know, Jim," he says, "is that the boy had absolutely no pulse." I guess I'll never know the final answer until eternity, and maybe that's a good thing, to keep me from taking any glory upon myself. And that's just fine with me—raising the dead has always been God's business, and God's alone.

Dead or not, the news of the boy's miraculous resuscitation spread across that city like wildfire, and the next night our meeting was bigger than ever.

The devil zero—God won!

Soon our medical doctor himself (his name was also Jim) was also involved in a miracle. During the day we would make visits to the villages in the area. In one village, a young man came running toward us, calling, "Doctor Jim needs you! Please come quickly!"

However, when we arrived, we found the good doctor standing in the yard of a mud hut holding a happy, grinning, vibrant baby about six months old.

Later he told us the story. He happened to be passing this hut, and suddenly the mother had rushed out of the hut, handed him the baby, and started to cry.

"That little fellow was burning up with fever," he told us. "He was very limp, and almost lifeless. I quickly sent a runner to find you so you could help us pray. And while I was waiting I began to pray and seek God's healing power."

And by the time we had arrived, we found the two of them enjoying each other's company, the child showing no signs of fever or sickness of any kind.

By the meeting's end, hundreds and hundreds of people had come forward in response to my call for full surrender to the Creator. We gathered on a muddy riverbank with water buffalo grazing nearby and onlookers everywhere, for a grand celebration of baptism.

My translator pastor—a young man in his 30s with huge muscles—stood waist deep in the murky water, lowering a young lady below the gentle waves. But then something strange happened. The pastor found that he could not lift that 90-pound woman to the surface again. She was being held under water and would soon be desperate for air.

From the shore I quickly spotted that something was not right, so I moved toward the water's edge. At the same time, with mighty power supplied by the Lord, the pastor managed to pull the woman above the water, but her body was contorted in strange gyrations and appeared to be in pain.

Two helpers carried her toward the shore. Without thinking about my next move, I met them and grabbed the woman by the shoulders with both hands. Holding her tight, I commanded the demons to come out of her in the name of Jesus Christ.

In a moment her contortions ceased and calm came over her. She wiped the water off her face, and slowly walked up the bank to her friends. The treacherous enemy of souls had attempted to drown her in the watery grave of baptism, but he was unsuccessful, and lost one more soul to heaven's kingdom.

Over the years, working in many countries of the world, I have come face-to-face with the devil as he seeks to destroy every shred of good which remains in humanity. Dear reader, I hope you realize that no matter where you live, *this battle is real, it is intense, and it is for keeps.* The deceiver knows he has a short time, and he is seeking to destroy everyone he can—you included! But our power and strength to overcome him can be found in the name of our King, who defeated the devil at every turn. And now He offers you and me the same power—if we choose to be led moment by moment by Him.

Throughout the above adventures I continued my journaling, a practice which drew me nearer and nearer to my blessed Lord. I never ceased praying, "Please, Lord, let me reach the world for you. You have done so much for me. I want to do all I can for you." The following words aren't original with me, but I wrote them in my Bible:

I want to do as much as I can
for as long as I can
for as many as I can
as often as I can.

Janene: Our adventures with Maranatha Volunteers have been the most exciting and fulfilling of my entire life. When I was young, I wanted to be a nurse, a teacher, or a dental assistant, but I was unable to pursue those dreams because of my family's financial situation. On our mission trips I have had the privilege of serving in each of those roles, and that of pharmacist as well. God has blessed me beyond my dreams.

I believe that everyone in North America, but especially our teens, will benefit from experiencing the joys of service in another country. When you visit a Third- or Fourth-World country, you see people and situations which cause you to say, "If not for the grace of God, there go I." And when you return to the U.S. or Canada and walk into your home, you will realize that God has blessed you far beyond what you deserve.

Jim: Overseas evangelism sometimes puts you into some unusual positions—and opens up some unexpected opportunities. One day I was glancing through an Adventist magazine and noticed an advertisement requesting evangelistic speakers in the Dominican Republic.

No way, I told myself as I studied the details. *This series will last a month, and I don't want to be gone from Janene that long.*

But I began to get the nagging feeling that the Lord wanted me on this mission trip. It didn't seem to promise anything different from trips I'd already been on, so why did I feel so strongly urged to go?

I talked it over with Janene. She told me, "If you're that impressed to go, you need to go." So I made the necessary arrangements, took the plane trip, and soon was immersed in the meetings, enjoying working with my new friend Pastor Freddie, the local Adventist minister.

One Monday about halfway through the series, Pastor Freddie asked me a question. "Jim, would you mind conducting a funeral for me?"

"Why can't you do it?" I replied.

"I've got so many things to do. It would be a big help to me if you'd take this one," he begged. "The family is having the service on a day that I'm not able to be there."

After a moment's thought, I said, "Sure, I'll do it."

The morning of the funeral, I asked the pastor a few questions. "Freddie," I said, "was this fellow a good man?"

"No," he replied. "People didn't like him."

I blinked." They didn't? Was he a Christian?"

"No, he wasn't a Christian," Freddie said. "In fact, he really wasn't a very good man."

Aha, I said to myself. *Now the light is starting to go on. Now I know why I was asked to take this funeral. Freddie didn't want to. But what am I going to do? What can I say about this man?*

The funeral was to be held in the family home, and when I arrived, the relatives escorted me to the position of honor—dead center behind the casket. (Well, maybe "dead" center isn't the best phrase to use.) There I was, my back to the wall and my belly almost touching the coffin. And to make it worse, the casket was open, and the old fellow was right there staring up at me waiting to see what I was going to say about him.

But I still didn't know. I didn't have a clue what to say. "Father, help me!" I prayed.

And help He did. I found myself suddenly launching into a sermon on the second coming of Christ. I spoke about those who die in the Lord being raised to life. (I didn't say anything about the others who would not.) I made a plea for those listening to me to be among that number who would be raised to life on that great day, and then I invited them to come to my nightly meetings. And that night, many of funeral guests showed up.

Later, my mind spun off in an interesting direction.

What about that dead man lying in that coffin? I wondered. *Since he wasn't a Christian, and apparently hated Christians, how did he like my message?*

He didn't say a thing, did he? Because he was dead. That reminds me of the apostle Paul's comment about living a victorious life in Christ. He said, "I die daily." There you have it. The Christian "dies" and allows Christ to live within themself. Think of it. A dead person never becomes upset over gossip, over somebody's bad driving, over a wife's or a husband's cutting remark, or over the boss's short temper—and the list could go on and on. You get my point, right? Nothing can offend a dead person.

In Philippians 2:5 Paul reminds us, "Let this mind be in you which was also in Christ Jesus." Jesus humbled Himself and became obedient to death. He surrendered all of Himself to the Father, and let the Father work His own will in Him. So the next time someone offends you or does something you dislike and you're tempted to yell, scream, or do anything stupid, think of the dead guy in the Dominican Republic. And if you do yell and scream—or whatever—ask your soul, "Have I died to self yet?"

Halfway through those Dominican meetings I had another sinister brush with demons. A woman with a pleasant personality came to me and asked if we could visit her at her home the next day. We agreed, and set a time. The following morning we arrived at her very humble dwelling.

"Please sit down," she said graciously, then launched into her story. "Every night when I go to bed," she said, "a tiny man runs into the bedroom. He jumps up on my bed, and while my husband is sleeping this little man tries to choke me."

"What do you think it is?" I asked.

"A demon," she responded. I agreed.

Since my first India crusade, I had become more familiar with demon possession, and had been led to cast out several more on subsequent trips. Don't get me wrong—it's not anything I go looking for.

"Would you pray with us?" I asked.

"I have never prayed before," she said, "and I have no idea how to do it."

I invited her to kneel, and asked her to repeat after me through the translator. This was one of the few times I have prayed while keeping my eyes open!

"Thank you, Lord, for your love," I prayed.

"Thank you, Lord, for your love," she repeated in her own language.

"I ask you for your help right now."

"I ask you for your help right now."

And then I said the words which I had learned would cause the devil to go crazy. If I was right, something was bound to happen.

"Lord," I prayed, "fill me with Your Holy Spirit, and may Your precious blood wash over me."

"Lord," she repeated, "fill me with Your Holy Spirit, and may Your precious —"

Wham! Suddenly she was slammed directly to the ground. I had my eyes open and I saw it happen.

Then she grabbed at her throat, a look of anguish and panic on her face. Her eyes were closed and her lips grimacing. Her fingers made prying motions as if to loosen unseen hands around her neck.

"Demons," I demanded, "come out of her in the name of the One who has all power—Jesus Christ. You must obey!"

Almost immediately the struggle was over. She opened her eyes and sat up.

"Are you all right?" I asked.

"I think so."

We finished our prayer, turning it into a prayer of thanksgiving, and the translator and I left. "I'll see you at the meeting this evening," I said.

Sure enough, she came to the meeting and the next night I asked her how she was doing.

"Everything is good," she said. "No more little man trying to choke me."

However, the following night she told me that she was still having problems and asked us to come back to her home.

I have learned that demons seek to gain entrance to a home and a person through items that have some demonic significance, such as pictures or carvings or masks of gods, and other mementos that may have satanic connections. When I learned this, I immediately threw away things I had kept from my old life such as my Turkish hookah (which I had used for a marijuana pipe). Eventually, I also threw away the carved demon heads I'd collected during my mission trips to various countries.

"Is there anything else in your life or in your home that may be connected to demons?" I asked the woman.

"Well," she said, "my husband believes in the dark arts, and when I have been sick he has taken me to the witch doctor for healing."

Our prayer time was an exact duplicate of the previous experience, and had the same results. The demon attacked, but after we sought God's help it stopped choking her.

Saturday night I preached my final sermon, and again gave a call for people to dedicate their lives to the Lord in baptism. Instead of coming forward, this woman left the room, although she had told me that she wanted to be baptized as soon as she and her husband could be married, which would happen soon.

At the closing night of the meetings we celebrated more baptisms, and when the local pastor finished immersing the final candidate, he gave his own call for a full commitment to serve the Lord, and for anyone who wanted to be baptized to stand. The woman, returning from outside, walked forward and stood on the marble floor in front of the baptismal font.

The pastor raised his hand and began to pray. *Wham!* The devil lifted her up almost perpendicular to the floor, and smashed her onto the marble. She thrashed violently, and immediately the elders jumped into action, pulling a large white curtain across the scene, hiding her from the view of the crowd who was then dismissed. Then each one grabbed an arm or a leg. Her face was turned away from me and she still thrashed violently.

"In the name of Jesus," I prayed, "Demons I demand that you come out of her. You cannot resist. You must depart from her in the name of Jesus Christ."

Then I did a strange thing which surprised me. I said, "Demons, I demand that you look at me."

In that brief moment time stood still as I watched her head whip toward me. Two black eyes like charcoal locked onto mine, and I found myself staring into the blackness of hell. Chills ran down my spine, and in that moment I was very thankful that I knew the Captain of the Lord of hosts.

"Demons," I repeated, "come out of her in the name of Jesus Christ. I command you to depart."

As quickly as it had begun, the struggle was now over, and she lay there in peaceful calm.

About a month later when I was back home, I received a letter from Pastor Freddie. His words brought joy and happiness to me. "Jim," he wrote, mentioning the woman's name, "we baptized her this week. The devil tried to drown her in the baptismal tank, but God got the victory! She is doing well."

On my flight home, I thought back over what had happened. *I still don't know why the Lord impressed me so strongly to do this Dominican Republic series,* I mused. *True, I've gained more experience—especially in dealing with demons—but was there some other reason?*

The answer came just a few hours later.

I landed in the Dallas-Fort Worth airport, and when I reached my next gate, there was Pastor Doug Batchelor of *Amazing Facts.* He was waiting for the same plane I was flying out on.

Chapter 21:

Wow!

Passing the time, we sat and talked about the evangelistic series I was returning from, and once he heard a bit more about my background, he asked me a question.

"Amazing Facts is planning a major satellite series from Cameroon in a little more than a year," he said. "We're going to need someone to do all of the on-the-ground organizing."

Well, isn't God amazing? He led me to do an evangelistic series in the Dominican Republic so I could meet up with Pastor Doug Batchelor in a Texas airport. A short time later, I received a phone call and soon I was Africa-bound.

I was eventually asked to join the Amazing Facts ministry full-time. My mind went back to the other time, years earlier, when I had rejected God's call to the ministry. But this time I didn't have a moment's hesitation. God had been working on me long and hard to bring me to the point where I could tell him, "Yes."

My eventual position with amazing facts was vice president for Public Affairs and Global Events. I was in charge of organizing many worldwide satellite evangelistic series, including some you may recognize or may have even participated in: *Visions for Life, The Prophecy Code, 04 Revival, 05 Revival,* and *The Most Amazing Prophecies.*

I had the privilege of writing a training manual called *Satellite Evangelism for the 21st Century,* which has been used in many locations around the world. In addition, hundreds if not thousands of churches have used my book *Reclaiming Lost Members* to train a church family in ways to reach hurting souls who no longer fellowship with them.

Speaking of family. One Sunday afternoon, during a break in my Amazing Facts work, I was sitting at home on our deck enjoying the day. I heard the phone ring inside and Janene's soft voice answering it.

Suddenly I realized that she was standing beside me on the deck, holding out the phone. "It's Sandi," she said. You might remember that Sandi was the woman I dated in college. She'd given birth to a baby boy many years before, and I believed I was the father.

"Hello?" I said, a question in my voice.

"Hi, Jim."

"Sandi. Hi. Why are you calling?"

"Jim, you're right."

"What am I right about?"

"Dan is your son after all."

This was a bombshell I had not expected after 34-plus years. I took a deep breath.

"OK," I said, feeling a bit dizzy. "OK. So why are you telling me this now?"

"Dan and his dad had a test done, and John is not his father. You are."

After some more conversation, we hung up. I called Dan, and soon I had a test of my own done, just to be sure. And yes indeed, I have another son—a son that the entire family, including my parents, wife, and children are thrilled about and have accepted with open arms! Although Dan lives in Washington state, we get to visit from time to time, and since my mom and dad live in Oregon, he gets to see them, too.

My years at Amazing Facts were wonderful ones. Among the many great things I was able to organize was an unprecedented evangelism/medical outreach to India. I love the people there so much, and it was a great joy to shepherd the project through to completion. We developed a cooperative effort between Amazing Facts, AMEN, and Maranatha Volunteers International. Eventually, our team consisted of almost 90 people from across the entire country, nearly half of them medical personnel.

None of us will know the final results of our efforts until we reach the heavenly shores, but I can give you the preliminary facts, which are nothing short of astounding. Thanks to all of our dedicated helpers, and to the Spirit of the Lord who inspired them, we treated 10,000 medical patients in 75 villages, and baptized almost 15,000 people into the family of God!

Remember my journal entry, "Lord, I want to reach the world for you"? Believe it or not, God had even more exciting things in store for me.

Janene: Jim had received several calls from other ministries, all of which we had been discussing and praying about. But when Dr. Benjamin Schoun called, I could tell things were different. All I could hear was Jim's side of the hour-long call, but when he hung up, I told him, "That's the call God wants us to take!" I paused, and then said, "Oh, by the way, who was on the phone?"

Jim stared at me in amazement. "You don't even know who I was talking to, and you think we should take the call?"

"Yes," I responded.

"Well, that was Adventist World Radio at the Seventh-day Adventist Church world headquarters in Silver Spring, Maryland," he continued, watching me closely. "And if we do go, that means we will need to move across the country."

"I know it will be a huge change," I said calmly, "but God is calling."

I've learned two huge things over the years. The first is that *when I give my life to God, I cannot say no,* and the second is that *God does not put a price on a soul He has decided I should reach, and neither should I.*

In a few days Jim had an official call, and in a week we were in Maryland looking for a home. In a month he was in his new office, and I was tying up loose ends in California, soon to follow.

Jim: This meant leaving our beloved northern California, all of our family, all of our friends, and the much-loved mountains we'd grown up in, to settle in the Washington, D.C., area where the mountains are no bigger than what we used to call "a little rise."

And did I mention that we would have to leave our horses? Well, they really aren't *my* horses—they're Janene's, and have been for years. The first time I kissed her was in front of her horse, and when I did, the horse gave me a dirty look! That was the start of many years of horses, Morgan horses, and lots of them. At one time we had around 20 head of every size, color, and shape. Well, that's a bit of an exaggeration, but you get the idea. Now, in addition to everything else we were leaving, Janene had to leave her beloved life with horses, too.

If you're a guy reading this, you won't really appreciate what I am saying, but I know the women will. Janene's horses were a big deal, a *very* big deal, but God had also been working on Janene just as much as he had on me. To this very day, I praise God that He worked on both of us and drew us to His side, together.

We prayed long and hard over the call we received, but in the end we both believed it to be what our Lord wanted us to do. So we packed up the truck and headed east. As is usual with God, it turned out to be far more than we ever imagined.

Chapter 22:

Working With Angels

Once I arrived at Adventist World Radio (AWR), I soon discovered it was one of the best-kept secrets in North America.

Why? Permit me to give you an enthusiastic two-paragraph infomercial.

AWR has an enormous gospel "footprint" which blankets much of the world for Christ. You can't pick up its signal easily in America and a few other Western-style cultures, but that's the point. AWR targets cultures that can't easily hear gospel broadcasting. At the time I'm writing this, it goes out in more than 80 major world languages, allowing us to reach a potential audience of 70 to 80 percent of the world's population.

AWR's shortwave signals reach across the restricted borders of, to name a few, North Korea, Iran, and Vietnam. It goes through prison walls, across borders, and beyond. Our FM and AM signals reach major centers of world commerce and into hearts everywhere. In the Soviet Union alone we air our message on more than 1,500 FM stations, reaching across 11 time zones. Our radio and Internet presence seeks out and changes lives in China and beyond. Our satellite flies like an angel of light across Central and South America, carrying the final message of hope.

Talk about answering the prayer, "Lord, help me reach the world for You."

I have the opportunity to share Christ around the world and not only in preaching. I get to write, produce, and host our TV series called *Making Waves*, which tells stories at least as dramatic as the ones you've read in this book.

Like the one about the AWR angel.

And yes, I mean a real angel.

Because it would be dangerous to the secret Christians who live there, I can't tell you the name of the country, but it's one that Christianity has barely penetrated until now. And its government has wanted to keep it that way. It's an extremely isolated area, made up of tribal people. The only religions they know are ancestral ones—they worship dead family members, trees, animals, and all sorts of other things. To show how serious the government is about keeping Christianity out, guards recently executed a man who tried to reach this area without getting proper permission. His horrified companion narrowly escaped through dense jungle with his own life.

Yet somehow word got out that, amazingly, a large number of these people were listening to Adventist World Radio. The radio waves had gotten past the soldiers, the police, the roadblocks, and all the efforts to keep these people from being "tainted" by influences from the outside world, especially Christianity.

But why were all these people suddenly tuning their shortwave radios to AWR? And where did they get radios?

Finally, one of our producers heard the answer from a reliable contact, someone who had somehow been able to sneak past the security police and enter a very large village. Once inside, he met with the chief—and found to his astonishment that there were thousands of people keeping the seventh-day Sabbath!

"But how can this be?" he asked the chief.

"Let me tell you what happened," the chief replied. "One day a very tall stranger came into our village. He was an imposing figure, and had an aura of light about him. He asked to see me. In his hand was a radio. He showed me how to use the radio, and then carefully showed me how to tune its dial to hear the Adventist World Radio program. He told me the frequency and the time the programs would be broadcast.

"'Share this with the entire village,' he said. 'It will be a great blessing to them.'

"I picked up the radio," the chief continued, "and turned to show it to someone who was with me. And as we turned back to thank the stranger, he was gone. We never saw him again, but we took this as a special sign that we should do what he said. We began to listen to the Adventist World Radio program, gathering around that radio every day."

Our contact told us that these village people are now devout believers. They keep the Sabbath, and worship while listening to the radio.

There are six different tribal villages in this mountainous region. None of them has any contact with each other because geographically they are very isolated. Our contact visited each chief in all six villages, and every chief told the same story without knowing what had happened in any of the other villages. They all described a very tall stranger, an imposing figure with an aura of light, carrying a radio and asking for the village chief.

Our AWR producer for this area says, "I must believe that this is the work of angels who care for these people. It seems unbelievable, but we must believe. I had goose bumps all over my body when I heard this report."

I hope that there may come a day when I will be able to interview these chiefs for our *Making Waves* series and hold the very radios that angels delivered.

Just recently, six *more* villages have been discovered keeping the Sabbath, and their chiefs tell the same story about the stranger with the aura of light.

Isn't that amazing? Angels are joining forces with the efforts of AWR to help complete the great commission given to us by Jesus to "Go into all the world and make disciples." After all, Jesus said, "And this gospel of the kingdom will be preached in all the world as a witness to all the nations, and then the end will come" (Matt. 24:14).

Can't you hear the footsteps of an approaching God? Can you turn on your TV or radio and not realize that the end is near—or the *beginning*, depending on how you view it?

We recently heard a remarkable story from the district pastor of the small, quiet village of Andravinambo, where the vanilla bean is grown, on the northeast coast of Madagascar.

A group of Adventists was traveling the countryside selling kitchen cooking pots. One day they arrived in Andravinambo to sell their wares. The Sabbath was approaching, so they asked the villagers, "Is there a Seventh-day Adventist church in the area?"

"No," said the villagers. "There is no Seventh-day Adventist church here."

Maybe these villagers aren't very familiar with the name of our denomination, the pot sellers wondered. So they asked the question another way:

"Is there a group of people who worship on Saturday?"

"Oh, yes," said the villagers. "There is one group that worships every Saturday, but they meet in a house and not a church."

"Can you show us where that house is?" asked the pot sellers.

When they arrived at the house on Sabbath morning, they saw an inscription hanging on the front: *The Seventh Day Keepers.*

The Adventists looked at each other, and hesitated. Someone inside noticed them, and came to the door and kindly beckoned them in. Once inside, they discovered about 50 people worshiping. As they listened to the teachings, following along in their Bibles, the Adventists thought, *These people look and sound just like us!*

After the meeting ended, they asked the leaders, "How did you come by your beliefs? How was your church formed?"

"Every day we listen to Adventist World Radio," one of the leaders said. "We have been convinced of the truth, and we have decided to follow God's will because we want to be ready for Jesus' second coming. We know that we need to keep Saturday holy, so we decided to worship God every Sabbath, and that is why we call ourselves The Seventh Day Keepers."

"But surely you have heard of Seventh-day Adventists," the pot sellers said. "From what we can see, you are teaching and preaching what Seventh-day Adventists believe."

The leader nodded. "But we did not want to use the name Adventist until we could meet a Seventh-day Adventist pastor who could tell us what to do to become a part of the Adventist church. So every week, we simply worship on Sabbath, and discuss Bible truth according to what we have learned through AWR."

I'm beginning to believe that I have the best job in the whole world—working for a team that is reaching the planet for Jesus Christ.

I recently heard of a girl I will call Nyle. This isn't her real name because she lives in a Muslim country where Christian believers must worship in secret, and where a slip of the tongue can mean prison or even death for a worshiper of Christ.

One day while twisting the tuning knob on her radio, Nyle discovered the AWR broadcasts. She began to secretly listen to them at night in her room, under cover of darkness. She not only listened regularly, but she soon fell in love with Jesus.

I dare not share my secret with my father, she told herself, *because he might kill me.* But she continued to study and grow in Christ, and after a while her conscience started to bother her. *I need to tell my father about the Savior,* she decided. *Even if he kills me, I am ready to die for my Lord.*

"Father, may I tell you something?" she asked him timidly one evening.

"What is it, my daughter?"

Cautiously, in a voice barely above a whisper, Nyle began to share her secret and the basics of her newfound life. When she finished, she held her breath, waiting to discover what fate awaited her.

As she fearfully watched her father's face, she was surprised to watch the corners of his lips turn slightly upward. *What does this strange expression mean?* she wondered. *It can't be a smile, because like other people in my country he hates Christians.*

For a moment, there was a dreadful curtain of silence, but it suddenly lifted as her father began to speak.

"My daughter," he said, "I have been keeping my own secret from you! I too was turning my radio dial one day, and I also found the Adventist World Radio broadcasts. I have been listening, and have fallen deeply in love with God. But I feared for my life. I was afraid to tell anyone in our family, including you."

WORKING WITH ANGELS

I was filming a *Making Waves* program in the far northeast area of India when I met one of our pastors who produces our radio programs there. He told me a story about our work among the animists. Animists worship the rocks, the sky, the animals, and—well, I guess you could say that they worship the creation rather than the Creator. It's a difficult and delicate task to introduce such people to the Creator God of the universe. But as I've learned, God customizes His appeals to fit every human heart.

One of the local women had acquired a well-paying government contract to raise silkworms, those little off-white creatures which look a lot like the mealworms we once fed our big aquarium fish at Jungle Jim's.

These little silkworms eat constantly. Their food of choice is large, freshly-picked mulberry leaves—fresh ones. That means that their owner can't simply pick leaves once a day, because the worms eat *four* times each day, and they won't touch anything except the freshest and most recently-picked leaves.

The worms are kept in flat boxes with two-inch high sides, open tops, and screened bottoms for air circulation. The mulberry leaves are harvested four times a day, and each time they must be finely chopped, and then sprinkled over the mass of tiny wrigglers.

Imagine the shock to her friends and neighbors when this woman accepted Christ. "I am going to begin keeping the Sabbath," she said, "and I am going to worship at the Seventh-day Adventist church."

"We didn't know you would ever become a Christian," one of her friends said, "let alone choose to attend a church which is almost a full day's journey from your home!"

"And this means certain disaster to your silkworm business," another warned. "Who is going to harvest the fresh leaves four times on Saturday? Who is going to chop them up and sprinkle them over the trays?"

"You're crazy," a third neighbor chimed in. "Your contract pays very good wages. Who in their right mind would turn away from financial security to serve a strange foreign God?"

"It doesn't matter," the woman said. "I'm going to church, and God will take care of me." And early the next Sabbath morning she disappeared over the hill.

The villagers talked things over among themselves. "Our friend has lost her mind," they decided. "We really need to help out with her silkworm business until she comes to her senses."

So after the woman had left for church, her friends went to the jungle with knives in hand, and harvested the mulberry leaves, then took them to the woman's house and chopped them up in fine pieces and sprinkled them over the trays.

A few hours later, carrying more newly-chopped leaves, they approached the silkworm trays again.

"That's strange," someone said. "The worms have not eaten what we brought this morning."

"Well, let's just sprinkle this new batch just in case," said another.

Afternoon shadows crept across the worm boxes as the neighbors returned a third time. They sprinkled the third meal of the day across the motionless creatures. "We've never seen anything like this before," they told each other. "The silkworms are sleeping. They've been sleeping all day long, and they've eaten nothing." Just to make sure, they brought leaves for the fourth meal of the day, but there was no change.

When the woman arrived home late Saturday night, her neighbors told her what happened. The next morning, and all through the week, her worms ate normally—but every Sabbath, they slept as a testimony to their Creator God!

Several pages back I mentioned that AWR's signal penetrates prison walls. And sometimes these signals have a dramatic effect.

One day in a tiny Hindu village a father and one of his sons were fighting over a small piece of land. No one knows the details of the dispute, but suddenly there was a scuffle, and the son broke the father's arm.

Enraged, the father clutched his broken arm and hurried off to tell his two other sons. "Look what your vicious brother has done to me!" he shouted.

"What do you want us to do?" they asked.

"You must go immediately and take care of him!"

So they went to visit their brother. During their discussion, voices and tempers raised, and one brother grabbed a machete and killed the one who had injured their father.

When the authorities heard about this, they immediately sentenced the father and both surviving sons to prison, leaving the women to fend for themselves, a very difficult challenge in India's culture.

In prison one son was given a radio, and one day while turning the dial to the BBC news he discovered Adventist World Radio. As he listened, he fell in love with Jesus Christ, committed his life to Him, and began to change. And he began to share his love for Jesus with the other prisoners, and many of them began to change as well, including his father and brother. The prison authorities were so impressed by this transformation that they gave the father and two sons a 40-day furlough to go to their home and visit the women they had left behind.

When the three arrived, the son who had listened to AWR located a radio and showed the family where to find the station. God began to work in the hearts and lives of these dear ladies, and it was not long before each of them decided to commit their lives fully to the Lord. On their own, without outside help, they began to keep the Sabbath and hold their own daily Bible studies and prayer time.

When I arrived with the *Making Waves* crew to film their story, the mother of the two sons told us, "Everything our hands find to do, God blesses. The crops produce more, the trees bear more fruit, the cows give more milk, and the water buffalo work harder."

We learned that God's blessings upon this family were so great that it was not long before the word spread to all the surrounding Hindu villages that there was a powerful Deity nearby. The stories kept coming . . . a woman traveled 10 kilometers to be healed of demon possession, and she found deliverance. Another woman came who, like the woman with an issue of blood for 12 years, could not find healing from any earthly source. Upon her arrival, she was healed.

Our crew had nearly finished filming, and we were about ready to leave.

"Could we all gather in a circle," I asked, "and have a prayer together?"

With cameras still rolling, and curious neighbors gathering around to listen, we began to pray. A moment later I heard a commotion to my left as a visitor fell to the ground, yelling and shaking her head. We stopped our prayer, grasped her by the shoulders, and demanded in the name of our Lord that the spirits leave her. In a moment, it was over, as God continued to cause this home to be a light upon the hill for this entire Hindu region. Since then the people continue to come and seek healing, deliverance, and peace of heart and mind in this Christian home—something that any other god simply cannot offer.

Wow! Talk about an answer to my prayer, "Lord help me to reach the world for you."

From a life of drugs, crime, and misery to a life of worldwide ministry. Our Lord is, indeed, God of the Second Chance!

I am so thankful that God was very patient with me, and never forgot my address. I praise Him that His forgiveness is wider than the universe and is free for the asking for all who will accept it . . . including me.

After reading my story, you can't possibly say that you have sinned too much for God to forgive you, or to be able eventually to work through you. God is ready to bless you more than you can imagine, in ways you can't possibly dream of.

"Eye has not seen, nor ear heard,
Nor have entered into the heart of man
The things which God has prepared for those who love Him."

Say yes to His Holy Spirit. And when you do—look out! The windows of the heavenly storehouse will open, and God will begin to rain torrents of blessings upon you.